The Icon
Through Western Eyes

The Icon
Through Western Eyes

Russell M. Hart

Templegate Publishers
Springfield, Illinois

Published in the United States of America in 1991 by:
Templegate Publishers
302 East Adams
P.O. Box 5152
Springfield, Illinois
62705

Manufactured in the United States of America

ISBN: 0-87243-186-X

DEDICATION

To my wife Dorene, whose encouragement I hope I never take for granted, I dedicate this book.

Contents

Icons of the Resurrection

Icons of Pentecost

FOREWORD

In recent months, as this book has begun to take shape, I have often asked the question, "Who needs it?" In part, I have needed the discipline of writing to identify some of the currents on my own spiritual journey, but also hope that this journey will be helpful to others. I do not wish to leave the impression that this journey is over. In fact, it may be just beginning. More than once in the process, a line from W.H. Auden's *The Quest* has popped into my head: "By standing stones the blind can feel their way."[1] If this book serves as a standing stone for one spiritual traveler, then it will have been worth the effort.

My journey began more than ten years ago as I was contemplating a doctoral project which would explore some avenues of approach to liturgical renewal within the denomination in which I am a minister. It was evident to me that the Church I served in Altoona, Pennsylvania, was in great need of renewal, and I hoped to acquire some tools which would make it happen. The congregation agreed to explore with me the Canonical Hours, and experimental liturgies that employed the five senses.

The project was an interesting failure. I understood correctly that liturgy — if it be genuine — must be the work of the people, but neither I nor my congregation came to terms with the fact that we cannot make worship happen. We tried, in a word, to stage-manage the Holy, and the Holy is far too elusive to be stage-managed. The one valuable thing I *did* learn is that if the divine-human encounter is to occur at all, it must be at the initiative of the divine. Even our reponse to the divine initiative is enabled by that same initiative. Every gathering of Christians, and every individual's devotional moment, becomes a potential time of "meeting." Either it happens, or it does not happen. It all depends upon the initiative of God.

9

In the process of experimenting with the five senses in worship, someone asked me if I had ever attended an Eastern Orthodox service. I hadn't. I assumed that the tradition had been a necessary developmental stage in the spiritual evolution of Christendom, the culmination being mainline Protestantism. I knew that the Eastern tradition was not exactly extinct, but thought it something of a spiritual dinosaur which had not yet been informed it was dead. Those were also the days immediately after Vatican II, and many of us believed that Rome would soon throw off the encrustations of the past, and be welcomed into the Protestant fold. Yet, in spite of this incredibly smug and grossly inaccurate view of church history, I had to admit that mainline Protestant worship — as it stood — seemed hollow. Yes, the hollowness was within me, but I was not willing to come to terms with that!

In the midst of the project, I was transferred to a parish in Harrisburg, a parish that turned out to have problems of its own. I completed the project which the new assignment had made somewhat irrelevant, and turned to other concerns.

Some time later, I made acquaintance with a man who I later discovered was an iconographer. One day, we were talking about art, and I asked him to explain the relationship between iconography and some of the great religious paintings, particularly those painted by El Greco. He explained that the icon was not "art" in the Western sense, but a "window to heaven." I replied that I thought it was all superstition. "No! It is not!" he responded with a determination that I found most unsettling.

His icons turned out to be austere and otherworldly as well as oddly compelling. My almost-forgotten conviction that genuine worship is a "point of meeting" may have prepared me to explore further what he had to say, because I found myself asking if I might try to paint an icon, and if he would teach me. He indicated that as I had not grown up in the Eastern tradition, I would have to meditate on the prototypes before I could begin to paint with any accuracy. The iconographic canon, he explained, had been set centuries ago, and the vocation of the iconographer is to transmit that tradition with as much accuracy as possible. There is little room, he continued, for the individual iconographer's flight of fancy. If a work is more reflective of the iconographer's impressions than of the tradition, it is not a icon.

I borrowed some prints of the Pantocrator[2] and agreed to meditate upon them until I was "ready" to paint. I thought that by "meditation" he meant "study" and study I did, until I was entirely satisfied that I could do the job. When he looked at my finished work, I sensed that he thought it was utterly awful, but he was kind enough to say that I was not yet conversant enough with the Byzantine style to be properly critical. It hung in my study for a while — just long enough for me to decide that it had to be banished to the attic, where it remains to this day.

Later that same year my wife and I took a Greek Island cruise. I hoped to see some of the "real" icons, but found that many of the village churches were filled with the same kind of lithographed devotional pictures as I had remembered from childhood. The museums, however, were another story. We found the Byzantine and the Benaki museums in Athens to be inexhaustible treasures. The Hosios Loukas Monastery chapel at Stiris holds some breathtaking tenth century mosaic icons, and a superb collection is preserved at the Monastery of St. John the Theologian on the island of Patmos.

I returned to Harrisburg determined to capture the Byzantine style even though it still eluded definition. I did not yet realize that it is *supposed* to elude definition because the Holy itself eludes definition.

I chose for my next subject a delicate Fourteenth Century icon of the twelve apostles.[3] My project, however, was soon to have a three-month interruption, for I was beginning to feel quite ill. I was informed that I had a debilitating and possibly life-threatening disease.

As the illness went through its stages I had no desire to think about icons at all. Gradually, however, the need for

11

rest subsided somewhat and I began to feel the isolation, frustration and anger that many sick people experience. Then came hours of self-reproach and anguish. I asked myself, "Was this like the agony of body and spirit that Jesus experienced in the wilderness of temptation?" I had assumed that meditation — when I finally discovered what it was — would be a pleasant experience. *This* was most unpleasant. In fact, it was hard and bitter agony.

One day I had a traumatic visit to the doctor's office. It was his "I'm going to be completely frank with you" speech. He told me quite frankly that I was going to have to live with certain limitations," and the sooner I accepted them, the better. When I returned to my sickroom I decided that dying would be better than being incapacitated and that if God wouldn't take my life, then I would do it for him. I prayed over and over, "Just let me die."

After awhile, it seemed that there was a benign, healing presence in the room — an energy that seemed to be coming from the icon of the twelve apostles. I was annoyed at this, but soon my annoyance gave way to curiosity. Shall I say, "A voice spoke"? It seemed to be saying, "Don't be so morbid. You're going to recover, and soon!" I cannot remember if I said anything aloud, but I remember thinking, "Prove it!" I found myself asking for a sign even though my theological training told me that this was the same sort of thing the pharisees were always asking of Jesus.

Immediately I felt stronger, and something like a voice said, "You have much to do before the time comes for you to die." I perceived that I was being told that I would be given sufficient energy to accomplish whatever God wanted me to do. That evening, when my wife returned from work, I announced that I was going to be better soon. She replied, "Of course you are, dear!" but I am certain that she didn't really believe it.

Once again, I began to work on the icon of the twelve apostles, and it seemed that the same benign, healing presence was there, giving me strength. Even though the very idea seemed ridiculous, I no longer knew or cared what was ridiculous and what was not. I was being healed. I knew it, and that was all that mattered.

It is entirely possible that I would have been cured in any case. It was the suddenness of the healing, and the fact that one month after the encounter I was once again competing in ten kilometer footraces that convinced me that God had in fact touched my life. For me, the icon had been the medium through which God had spoken.

From that day forward I knew I would continue to paint — or, as the Greeks say, to "write" icons. As far as I am concerned, preparing to deliver a sermon, and preparing to paint an icon are part of the same process. We Protestants believe that the Word preached is a means whereby God communicates with the faithful. I have come to believe that this same Word is encountered in the icon.

Some months ago I was introduced to a Greek Orthodox priest — Fr. John Chakos of Pittsburgh. He inquired about my iconography and said that he found it curious that a United Methodist minister would *be* an iconographer. I admitted that I found it rather odd myself and that I realized that only Orthodox Christians could be iconographers. He smiled and replied, "Let God decide."

This book is an expression of my desire to share my journey and some of its fruit. I am convinced that Orthodoxy has something precious to share with the rest of Christ's Church, especially the heirs of the Reformation. This is my offering in what I hope will be the continuation of a dialogue that is still in its infancy. We have much to learn from one another, much to share, and much yet to receive from the Source — the source of all goodness and beauty, truth, and love.

---

1   Auden, W.H., *Selected Poetry of W.H. Auden,* Modern Library/Random House, New York, 1958., p. 61.

2   Pantocrator: Lit. "Ruler of All." This icon, found in the dome of Orthodox churches, is of Christ holding the Gospel in one hand, while extending a blessing with the other.

3   Weitzmann, Kurt, The Icon: *Holy Images — Sixth to Fourteenth Century,* George Braziller, Inc., One Park Ave., NY., 10016, p. 122.

The Holy Face

This icon was written by John Barns and is used
with his permission.

ICONS AND THEIR MEANING

The word *icon* is simply a Greek word meaning "image" or "portrait," and as such, refers to a representation of a holy person, whether on a painted panel, bas-relief, or sculpture in the round. Because of the popularity, among Christians of the East, of painted panels for private devotions, the word *icon* is no longer used to refer to any other type of art than this sort of representation.

It is impossible to ascertain when the painted image was first used by Christians as a means of devotion. Leonid Ouspensky, in his book *Theology of the Icon* argues that it evolved from funerary frescoes in the Roman catacombs. If this is true, the painted image has been part of Christian tradition from the inception of the faith. It is also certainly true that opposition to painted images is at least as old as the images themselves. This opposition can be traced in part to the Old Testament prohibition of images, the Jewish antipathy toward the painted image, and the fact that the Eastern Church, being a part of the Byzantine Empire, found itself being gradually displaced by Islam. Among Muslims, opposition to any depiction of the human form in worship was, and remains, uncompromising. The Empire fell to the Turks in 1453, but by then the iconographic tradition was firmly established in Russia, where it perhaps enjoyed its greatest flowering.

The greatest threat to the icon, however, came from within the Eastern Church itself. This came in the form of the "Iconoclastic Controversy," which raged from 725 to 842 A.D. It began, largely due to the influence of Leo III the Isaurian who, in an Imperial edict, declared all icons to be idols and ordered their destruction. It ended with the death of the Emperor Theophilos, whose widow, Theodora, saw to it that the monk Methodios was elected Patriarch. Since 842 A.D., on the first Sunday of Lent, the Orthodox have observed a feast called "The Triumph of Orthodoxy," in

17

commemoration of that day when the veneration of icons was reestablished. Since that time, the icon has been an integral part of Orthodox tradition.

John of Damascus wrote a treatise entitled *Defense of Holy Images* prior to the worst excesses of the controversy, in which he agreed with the adversaries of icons that God, being invisible, and inconceivable, could not be represented. But because God had, through Christ, become man, Christ can — indeed must — be depicted in human form for the sake of our salvation.[1] This defense, based in part on Col. 1:15 — "He is the image (icon) of the unseen God," — elevated the icon to an importance equal to the written Word, the appeal to the ears. Luke 10:23-24 is also cited as an authentication of this point of view. "Blessed the eyes that see what you see, for I tell you that many prophets and kings longed to see what you see but never saw it; to hear what you hear but never heard it." I John 1:1 is also cited. "That which has existed since the beginning, that we have heard, that we have seen with our own eyes, that we have touched with our own hands: the Word who is life — this is our message."

Leonid Ouspensky tells us that the Orthodox believe that the icon "corresponds entirely to the 'word' of scripture. That which the word communicates by sound, the painting shows silently by representation."[2]

In addition to Christ and the saints, Orthodox iconography includes a pictorial cycle of the twelve feasts called the Dodecaorton. These include: the Annunciation, the Nativity, the Presentation in the Temple, Christ's Baptism, the Transfiguration, the Raising of Lazarus, the Entry into Jerusalem, the Crucifixion, the Harrowing of Hell, the Ascension, Pentecost and the Death of the Virgin. This latter icon, though not grounded in Scripture, is grounded on sacred tradition.

The first icon — the earliest — according to Orthodox tradition, is the icon of the Holy Face. This image is reputed to have originated as a life-portrait of the Savior. This story, which is admittedly legendary, gives us insight into a tradition which, if it does not extend back to the time of the Apostles, is still from the formative years of the faith.

Abgar, so the story goes, was king of Edessa and a leper. Having heard of the miracles of Christ, he sent his archivist Ananias with a letter requesting Christ to come to Edessa and heal him. Ananias was a painter, and Abgar instructed him at least to make a portrait of the Savior in case he declined to come.

Ananias did attempt a portrait, but because Christ was surrounded by a great crowd, and because of the indescribable glory of his face which kept changing through grace, Ananias was unable to complete the task. Seeing that he was having difficulty, Christ asked for some water, wiped his face with a wet linen towel and his features were imprinted on the cloth.

As Abgar had guessed, Christ refused to go to Edessa, as he had a mission to fulfill, but promised, once the mission was completed, to send one of the disciples in his place.

When he received the portrait, Abgar was healed, but not completely. After the Ascension, Thaddeus went to Edessa, completely healed the king and converted him to the faith. Abgar removed an idol from its niche above the gate of the town and replaced it with the holy image, and devoted the rest of his reign to spreading Christianity throughout his kingdom.

Later, a grandson, who was a pagan, became king and would have destroyed the image, but the bishop of the town had it bricked into its niche, after placing a burning lamp before it. The image was soon forgotten altogether.

In 544 A.D., during a Persian siege of the town, a bishop was shown its hiding place in a dream. He uncovered the image and found that the lamp was still burning. In addition, the image had been imprinted on the inner side of the tiles which had concealed it. By virtue of the image, the siege was lifted and the town was spared.

In 630 A.D., the Muslims seized Edessa, but did not forbid veneration of the image. In 944 the Emperor had it brought to Constantinople at the price of two hundred Saracen prisoners, 12,000 denarii of silver and the promise that Imperial troops would never attack the city nor its surrounding lands.

The image which had survived paganism and the Muslims did not, apparently, survive the Crusaders. In 1204 A.D., it disappeared during the sack of Constantinople. It had been, however, frequently reproduced, and every extant icon of the Holy Face is said to have been derived from the prototype.[3]

With this background, we turn to Ouspensky's restatement of Orthodox dogma on the subject:

> ..truth is a person, and it has an image. This is why the Church not only speaks of the truth, but also shows the truth: the image of Jesus Christ.[4]

The Orthodox also believe that the first images of the Virgin Mary were painted from life by St. Luke, and also that likenessess of the saints were made while they were still alive, or at least before memory of their likenesses was lost.

The iconographic style — sometimes called the "Byzantine" style — is strange to Western eyes and may even appear crude or ugly. It also seems to betray a primitive understanding of perspective. But the integrity of the "style" gradually reveals itself to the person who takes the time and effort to try to understand what it means to convey.

One of the goals of the iconographer is to achieve "laconism" that is, to reduce the image to a minimum of details to achieve a maximum of expression.[5] The icon is laconic as the scripture itself is laconic — revealing only what the writer intended to convey and nothing more. Icons are sober as scripture itself is sober. Details are tolerated only when they have some spiritual significance.

The iconographer attempts to purify his or her art of all

individual elements.[6] If this is never wholly achieved, there still remains an astounding uniformity among icons painted over the centuries. They are never signed, because it is the first concern of the iconographer to pass on the Tradition and to set his or her own "style" aside.

Icons are not intended to be viewed as art. They address the viewer, or rather, engage the viewer as scripture engages the reader or the hearer.

While the icon preserves the physical peculiarities of the person depicted, it shows — not the earthly countenance as does a portrait — but his or her "glorified, eternal face."[7]

An excessively thin nose, a small mouth and large eyes — these convey the inner state of a person whose senses have been refined i.e., transfigured through grace.[8]

The ancient liturgy of St. James well expresses what the icon attempts to convey:

> Let all mortal flesh keep silence,
> And with fear and trembling stand;
> Ponder nothing earthly minded,
> For with blessing in his hand,
> Christ our God to earth descendeth,
> Our full homage to demand.[9]

The icon never strives to "stir the emotions of the faithful. Its task is not to provoke in them one or another natural human emotion, but to guide every emotion as well as the reason and all the other faculties of human nature on the way to transfiguration."[10]

In the icon there is no single light source, as one finds in Western art, where light illuminates objects from one side or another. Iconographic technique depicts the divine light of the kingdom of God which permeates all things and casts no shadows. For the iconographer, light becomes the "background" of the icon.[11] Where gold leaf is used, light appears to radiate from the icon itself. The halo is defined as "an external expression of the transfigured state of man, of his sanctification by uncreated divine light."[12] The halo expresses a state of grace which defies representation, and which is perceived only through grace. Holiness has no external characteristics. During his lifetime, the holiness of the Lord was perceived only through the gift of grace. "The world," says the Metropolitan Philaret, "does not see the saints as the blind do not see the light."[13]

The architectural forms which often compose the background of the icon seem baffling to Western eyes. One assumes that because the iconographer ignores the laws of perspective, he or she must be ignorant of them. It has also led many casual observers to conclude that the icon is primitive. Doors lead nowhere. Walls do not seem to stand of their own weight, and columns do not even support themselves, let alone fulfill their customary function. The iconographer uses these fanciful architectural forms to show that the action taking place before our eyes is not bound by the limitations of human logic, but occurs in a realm where the laws and logic of earthly life are suspended.[14] This action always occurs in the out of doors. This tells us that no human structure can "contain" the Incarnation and that in the Kingdom of God, nothing is hidden. When scripture indicates that the action depicted in the icon *did* occur indoors i.e., in the Temple or the Upper Room, a drapery is usually suspended between two architectural forms, but again, this is only a background device, and is incidental to the action taking place within the icon.

The icon does employ perspective of a sort, but this is an inverse perspective which seems to surround the viewer. In inverse perspective, the point of departure "..lies, not in the depth of the image, but in front of the image, as it were in the spectator himself."[15]

The Western mind, if it is to understand the theology of the icon, must begin with the Transfiguration of Christ, where his divine nature was revealed to Peter, James and John in a mystical experience on the mountain. The Orthodox believe that the faithful man or woman *can* reestablish through grace the divine image disfigured as a consequence of the Fall. The man or woman of faith can be transformed by internal effort into a "living icon of Christ".[16]

Ouspensky states the divine purpose of the Incarnation with great precision:

> The dogma of the divine incarnation has two aspects:

> 'God became man so that man could become God.' On the one hand, God comes into the world, participates in its history; lives among us; on the other hand, there is the purpose and meaning of the Incarnation: the deification of man, and through this, the deification of all creation, the building up of the 'Kingdom to come,' and this is the reason for its existence. This is why everything in the Church converges toward this aim — all life, all activity, all manifestation of human creativity, including artistic creativity.[17]

For Protestants, the primary article of faith is that divine truth is revealed in the Word. The Orthodox believe this, but also believe that since the Word is made flesh, it is revealed through the divine image, and through this revelation the divine image effaced by the Fall is even now being restored through faith, and through the works of faithful men and women.

Orthodoxy has demonstrated a staying power for nearly two millenia, and often in lands hostile to it. This is particularly true in the Soviet Union where for seventy years it endured a persecution unparalleled since the time of the Roman Empire.

The Protestant West retains a suspicion of images which has been part of its very fabric since the time of the Reformation. This does not mean, however, that the artistic representations of Christ, other Biblical characters and church leaders are absent from Protestant houses of worship. But having no Tradition to follow, much "Protestant" art has followed the conventions of the age, and thus has a superficial character when it is new, and appears sentimental when conventions and taste change.

Yet art, even "bad" art, is a powerful communicator. Its power may be equal to, or greater than the power of the Word preached. The question which must be asked is, "What is being communicated?" Protestant tradition has elevated proclamation to an art form. There are exacting standards for sermon prepartion and delivery. The Church finds it difficult to tolerate "bad" preaching, but seems to have a great capacity for the toleration of "bad" art.

If the "visual" *is* a means of receiving revealed truth — perhaps the time has come for Protestants to entertain the possibility that Orthodoxy has something to say to us, or rather, something to *show* us.

1   Weitzmann, Kurt, *The Icon,* George Braziller, NY., 1978, p. 8.
2   Ouspensky, Leonid, Theology of the Icon, St. Vladimir's Seminary Press., Crestwood, NY 10707., 1978., p. 10.
3   Ibid., pp. 59-62.
4   Ibid., p. 117.
5   Ibid., p. 97.
6   Ibid., p. 97.
7   Ouspensky, Leonid and Lossky, Vladimir, *The Meaning of Icons,* St. Vladimir's Seminary Press, Crestwood, NY 10707., 1982., p. 39.
8   Ibid., p. 38.
9   The Book of Hymns, The United Methodist Publishing House, Nashville., 1964., #324.
10 Op. Cit., Ouspensky., p. 39.
11 Ibid., p. 40.
12 Ibid., p. 38.
13 Ibid., p. 38.
14 Ibid., p. 41.
15 Ibid., p. 40.
16 Op. Cit., *Theology of the Icon,* p. 193.
17 Ibid., p. 174.

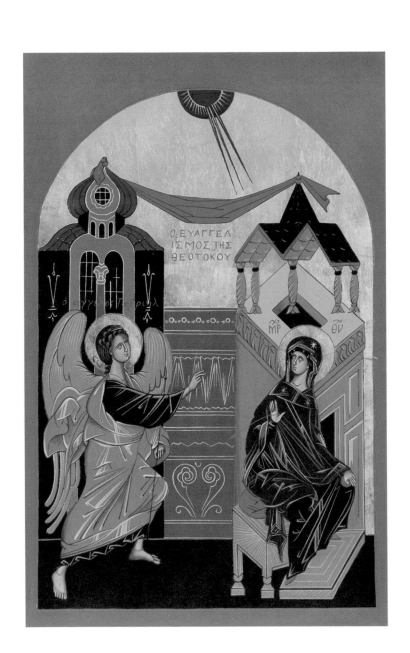

THE ANNUNCIATION

> Today is the fountainhead of our salvation and the
> revelation of the mystery that was planned from
> all eternity: The Son of God becomes the Son of
> the Virgin and Gabriel announces this grace. Let
> us join him in crying out to the Mother of God:
> 'Hail, O Woman, full of grace! The Lord is with
> you.'[1]

Luke's account of the Annunciation, like the rest of his
nativity cycle, is a superb example of laconic prose. No
superfluous detail is allowed. Only that which is essential remains. This same "laconism" reflects—as I have already indicated—the goal of the iconographer, and is perhaps
nowhere better executed than in the icon of the Annunciation.

Gabriel ("Hero of God") is the messenger. If we are put
off by his presence, it may be because we as Protestants tend
to regard angels as part of the department store trivia that
helps the merchants sell us this world's goods at Christmas.

In the most ancient texts, the Angel of Yahweh is not a
created being (Gen. 16:7), but God in a form visible to his
creatures. The presence of Gabriel links the Annunciation to
the prophets and the apocalyptic imagery of the Old Testament. When Gabriel appears in the book of Daniel (9:21), he
is the vehicle of revelation.

In the icon he is represented as a winged being.
Iconographic tradition uses this symbol to convey the
divine origin and urgency of the Word.

Woe to anyone who encounters the messenger of the
Word and is not prepared to receive it! Zechariah was not
prepared to receive the prophecy concerning the birth of
his son, John the Baptist, and was struck dumb. Mary had
the grace to receive the messenger and the Word, and was
thus blessed.

Most icons of the Annunciation depict Gabriel as running. He has just "descended from heaven and his look is the look of a diligent servant carrying out the task given him by his master."[2] In his left hand he holds the staff of a messenger, and his right hand is extended almost as though he holds an invisible baton. Mary turns toward him in complete surprise, dropping the purple yarn she has been spinning. She gazes, however, not upon the messenger but toward heaven. Gabriel himself looks toward heaven, indicating that the message is not his own, but comes from God the Father.

Luke tells us that the Son of God is to be conceived by a human mother—a virgin in accordance with the Old Testament prophecy as the Church read it in the Greek text of Isaiah 7:14. The angel's greeting identifies Mary as that virgin in his words, "Rejoice, highly favored one! The Lord is with you" (Luke 1:29).

Mary the highly favored is literally "the graced one." She is the culmination of the history of Israel as Paul indicates in Galatians 4:4, "...but when the appointed time came, God sent his son on a mission to us. He was born of a woman, born subject to the Law. He was to ransom those who were under the Law that we might receive the adoption of sons."

John Macquarrie reflects on the intent of this text with these words:

> In the beginning, or even before the beginning, God conceived humanity as his child and partner. So he purposed to bring the human race into loving communion with himself, and he purposed to do this by himself assuming humanity and tabernacling with his people (John 1:14). He must then also have purposed to bring the human race to the moment when it had been so cleared of sin and filled with grace that it would be ready to receive the gift of himself. That moment in the history of humanity was Mary.[3]

For the Orthodox, Mary represents a real transformation of human nature, "progressively purified and raised up by grace during previous generations."[4] This is not as far removed from the historic doctrines of Methodism as one might think, for John Wesley believed that the Gospel was given by God to change the hearts and minds of his children—so completely as to make them holy. This belief is called the doctrine of Christian Perfection. It claims that we *can* be made perfect through grace in *this* life and share in the divine nature (2 Peter 1:4).

Although Wesley makes few direct references to Mary, in his *A Letter to a Roman Catholic,* he says this about her: "I believe that he was made man, joining the human nature with the divine in one person, being conceived by the singular operation of the Holy Ghost and born of the Blessed Virgin Mary, who, as well after as she brought him forth, continued a pure and unspotted virgin."[5] What made her blessed? Was it her obedience? Was it her humility? Was it her submission? One wonders whether Wesley might be indicating that Mary is a type of "firstfruits" of perfection.

To be grace-filled is to be in the opposite condition from that of original sin, which we may define as the environment of disobedience which creates the alienation of human life. This process was set in motion when the first of God's children said, "My will be done!" This, the Orthodox explain, was stated in the disobedience of the first Eve. But in the East, original sin is not seen as inherited guilt, but a weakening of the will which has accompanied—as well as caused—the disfigurement of the Divine image in creation. This weakening, however, is not believed to have abolished humankind's basic freedom to choose good rather than evil.[6] Mary, unlike her sister Eve, was so grace-filled that all channels were open. The fullness of time had arrived. The moment was ripe for the Incarnation.

Luke tells us that the Word of God and the presence of the messenger filled Mary with perplexity, as any encounter with the holy fills the recipient with fascination mingled

31

with fear. The angel said, "Mary, fear not; you have found favor with God. You shall conceive and bear a son and you shall call him Jesus. He shall be called the Son of the Most High. The Lord God will give him the throne of his father David; he will rule over the house of Jacob forever and his reign will have no end" (1:31-33).

"Son of the Most High" is a title that God would bestow on the Messiah as conceived by the Jewish national hope. It does not convey the idea of physical or metaphysical relationship as does "Son of God" in verse 35. Luke is saying in this contrast that Christ will not only fulfill the Jewish national hope but will supercede that hope. He will be the Word foretold by the prophets but will not be contained by that Word. He will be for the Greeks, that is, for the gentiles as well as the Jews. Prophecy itself anticipated this fulfillment, this overflowing of the old vessels. For, "..great is his dominion in a peace without end" (Isaiah 9:6-7).

Persons who do not perceive the presence of the holy in their own lives cannot be prepared for the enormity of what the angel says next. Mary, however, was prepared. From her girlhood she had been taught that one spot on earth was to be venerated above all other. This spot was the heart of Judaism. It was the Temple at Jerusalem. In that temple there was another place, a place so holy that only the High Priest could enter and he only once a year, to atone for the sins of the nation.[7] She must have realized that the same glory of God—the *Shekinah*—which had filled the tabernacle in the wilderness, and which Ezekiel had envisioned leaving and returning to the temple, would now cover her with its shadow.[8]

Those who see the doctrine of the Virgin Birth primarily as a bulwark defending the inerrancy of scripture surely miss the awesome nature of the pronouncement "..the power of the Most High will overshadow you" (Luke 1:35). The very glory of God would rest upon her and within her. She would become a "living temple." The great Athanasius once wrote:

> For being himself mighty and artificer of everything, he prepares the body of a virgin as a temple unto himself, and makes it his very own as an instrument, in it manifested and in it dwelling.[9]

It is not my intention to claim some sort of "deity" for Mary. If God's spirit rests upon her and within her, it also rests upon and within any Christian man or woman who says, "Let it be done according to your Word." This is what Paul means when he says, "Did you not realize that you were the temple of God and that the Spirit of God was living among you?" (I Corinthians 3:16). As Protestants, we can appreciate Mary best when we see her as a model for our own obedience.

Mary is a woman of faith. She does not ask for a sign as Zechariah had done (Luke 1:18). Nevertheless a sign is given. Elizabeth, like Sarah before her, is pregnant in her old age. The theme of Genesis 18:14 repeats itself. Nothing is impossible with God.

Mary's answer, "I am the handmaid of the Lord, let it be done to me as you have said." (Luke 1:18) is the very heart of the doctrine of the incarnation and the heart of the Protestant problem. Fr. Daniel Flanagan asks, "Does the incarnation say something specific about Christ only, or about man? If so, what does it say?"[10] In the spirit of the Wesleyan doctrine of prevenient grace, Flanagan states the conviction that man — or woman — is capable of receiving a genuine sanctifying grace the moment he or she utters Mary's fiat, "Let it be done to me as you have said."

Karl Barth says, "No!" to this. He says that this implies creaturely cooperation in God's revelation and reconciliation. It is, he believes, a "spurious" problem, "..the sole answer to which can be false doctrine."[11]

I remember an earnest young man who began to attend one of my churches. He involved himself in the Sunday School, the choir, the Wednesday night prayer group and the youth program. I began to become concerned that he might "burn out." In time he began to manifest some of the signs. He became sharply critical of the denomination's Sunday School curriculum and, increasingly, what he heard from the pulpit. On World Communion Sunday, we celebrated the sacrament for the first time with a common chalice and loaf. He was used to the more conventional form with the individual communion glasses and cubes of bread. At the conclusion of the service he assailed me with these words, "How dare you use those 'Catholic' practices!" I explained that the communion service can be celebrated a variety of ways. At that moment, what was really bothering him boiled to the surface. "You seem," he exploded, "to be saying that sinners have something going for them!" "They have!" I replied. "It is called the grace of God!" I never saw him again. That vestige of the doctrine of Total Depravity seems to be at the heart of the Protestant problem with Mary. For many, it seems close to blasphemy to entertain the idea that God should call his creature into service and give her (or him) part of his overwhelming generosity, or that God in his absolute autonomy might consent to be dependent."[12]

Cardinal Suenens asks, "Is it inconceivable that God, by the Archangel Gabriel, should require Mary's consent? Is it beneath Him to await her answer?"[13] It seems to me that the former question would require a resounding "Yes," and the latter an unqualified "No."

Alan Clark suggests that the Son of God owes a creature's debt to his mother. "If the son is sensitive as no other man has ever been sensitive, then he learnt that sensitivity from his mother. For clearly, she 'sends' him on his way and supports him from the shadows, undemanding, perhaps at times uncomprehending."[14] Clearly, God needs the obedience of his creatures to work out his purposes.

The position of the Orthodox East since the Council of Ephesus (431 AD) has been that Mary is the Theotokos — the Mother of God. Christ took human nature from his mother, and because he who took human nature is God, Mary is the

Mother of God. He was God living a human life and not just a man who "knew" God, or with whom God was intimately associated. Mary is unique among God's creatures because through her obedience, God began to restore his lost creation to its original state of grace.

Mary is the "firstfruits" of the perfection to which God calls each of his creatures — a perfection expressed in Wesley's doctrine of Christian Perfection and in the sublime hymnody of his brother Charles:

> Christ, by highest heaven adored;
> Christ, the everlasting Lord!
> Late in time behold him come,
> Offspring of the virgin's womb.
> Veiled in flesh the Godhead see;
> Hail th'incarnate deity
> Pleased as man with me to dwell,
> Jesus, our Emmanuel.

> Hail the heaven-born Prince of Peace!
> Hail the Sun of Righteousness!
> Light and life to all he brings,
> Risen with healing in his wings.
> Mild he lays his glory by,
> Born that man no more may die,
> Born to raise the sons of earth,
> Born to give them second birth.[15]

Or this:

> Visit, then, this soul of mine;
> Pierce the gloom of sin and grief;
> Fill me, Radiancy divine;
> Scatter all my unbelief;
> More and more thyself display,
> Shining to the perfect day.[16]

Mary's fiat permits the "sons (and daughters) of earth" to be raised to "second birth." The Incarnation—the fruit of Mary's obedience—permits "this soul of mine," to be filled with "radiancy divine," shining until the "perfect day" wherein we are restored by faith to our lost state of grace.

This psalm of praise, chanted at the Orthodox Feast of the Annunciation, has much the same content as the Wesley hymns:

> ..She answered and said: 'Be it done to me according to your word and I will give birth to the Bodiless one who will take flesh from me, so that by his union with a body, man may be raised to the original state of grace, for He is mighty.[17]

1   *Byzantine Daily Worship,* Alleluia Press, PO Box 103, Allendale NJ., 07401. 1969., p. 658. Troparion (Fourth Tone).

2   Ouspensky, Leonid and Lossky, Vladimir, *The Meaning of Icons,* St. Vladimir's Press., 1952., p. 172.

3   Stacpoole, Alberic, O.S.B., Editor, *Mary's Place in Christian Dialogue,* Morehouse-Barlow Co., Inc., Wilton Connecticut., 06897., 1982., p. 99.

4   Ibid., p. 177.

5   Outler, Albert C., Editor, *John Wesley,* Oxford University Press, NY., 1964., pp. 494-495.

6   Op. Cit., p. 177.

7   Ibid., p. 73.

8   Ibid., p. 73.

9   From *Christology of the Later Fathers,* Vol. III, The Library of Christian Classics, ed. by Edward Rochie Hardy and Cyril C. Richardson, 62-63. Published in the USA by the Westminster Press, 1954. Cited by Pfatteicher, Philip H., *Festivals and Commemorations,* Augsburg Publishing House, Minneapolis, 1980., pp. 133-134.

10 Op. Cit., p. 20.

11 Church Dogmatics, II, 2, pp. 143-144., as cited by Stacpoole, Alberic, O.S.B., Editor, *Mary's Place in Christian Dialogue.*

12 Ibid., p. 73.

13 Ibid., p. 73.

14 Ibid., p. 84.

15 *The Methodist Hymnal.,* The Methodist Publishing House, Nashville, TN., 1964., #387.

16 Ibid., #401.

17 Op. Cit., Byzantine Daily Worship., p. 659.

THE NATIVITY

Today the Virgin gives birth to the One who surpasses all essences, and the earth offers a cave to God, the Inaccessible One. Angels sing his glory together with the shepherds: for to us is born a Child, God in all eternity.[1]

Every Christmas season for a decade I took Holy Communion to an elderly woman whose meager household consisted of a kitchen, a dining room which held her bed, and a sitting room. I cannot say that she was "religious" in the pious sense. She was simply old and infirm and thus on my list of "stops." Every year she would have her son set up the train table which held the artificial Christmas tree and "Santa's village." The neighborhood children looked forward to it and this meant company for her.

On the other side of the room, as far away from the tree assemblage as the room would allow, she placed her creche. I don't suppose I noticed the significance of this until later. Now I suspect that she believed that *this* assemblage, unlike the other one, was "different." Even the children may have sensed it. I noticed that at the train table they were self-absorbed and jostled one another. But at the creche, they were diffident, their self-absorption turning to self-consciousness, even shyness.

There in that modest room was seen the paradox of the Incarnation. It has abolished the separation between the sacred and the profane, yet the sacred is not de-sacralized, is not diminished. The profane, however, is ennobled, redeemed, and "raised." It appears the same as before, it is true, but it can never be the same again. It is drawn, imperceptibly to the Light, until it is transformed by it. This is the message of the icon of the Nativity.

The earliest examples of this prototype are at least as old as the Fifth Century. The composition was the decorative motif engraved on small oil flasks obtained by pilgrims at Bethlehem's Church of the Nativity. The composition reveals the essence of the event of the Incarnation, its effect on the natural world, and a perspective of its consequences.[2] St. Gregory captures the essence of the Nativity for the Orthodox in one sentence: "(It) is not a festival of creation, but a festival of re-creation, of a renewal, which sanctifies the whole world."[3] Through the Incarnation of God, the whole created order acquires its true meaning and the purpose of its being—Transfiguration, or as Wesleyan theology understands it, the possibility of Perfection.

In the icon, the representatives of the created order render service, as expressed in this ancient liturgical psalm:

> O Christ, what shall we offer you for your coming on earth as a Man for our sake? Every creature that has its being from you gives thanks to You: the angels offer hymns of praise, the heavens give a star; wise men present their gifts and the shepherds their wonder; the earth provides a cave and the desert a manger. As for us, we offer You a Mother, a Virgin Mother.[4]

The angels, who are representatives of the heavenly host, perform a twofold service: they glorify God and bring good tidings to the world. In this icon, some turn their heads toward the heavenly sphere and sing the Glory of God, while others lean downward to the shepherds.[5] These messengers of God, Orthodox tradition dictates, are part of the created order. Perhaps a difficulty may be avoided here if we simply say that they represent the presence of God in a form discernible to his creatures. The first response of the shepherds is outright fear, then wonder and amazement. They are not struck dumb as Zechariah, but themselves sing praise to the babe.

These shepherds, like Mary herself, are the *anawim,* the righteous poor. Unlike the magi, who must be led by the light of reason, they are led by direct experience, amid their everyday working life. One shepherd expresses wonder at the message of the angel while another plays a tune on his shepherd's pipe, adding a human paean of praise to the celestial chorus. These humble folk represent believing Israel.

The heavenly sphere, placed at the top center portion of the icon, is an opening to the world beyond. This same sphere appears in the icons of the Baptism of Christ, the Transfiguration, and the Harrowing of Hell. In this icon, a long ray from the star points directly to the cave. This star is no mere celestial phenomenon as the Christmas planetarium shows would indicate, but a messenger from the world of Uncreated Light, signifying that in the Incarnation, the Almighty God has come very near. The star, like the angels, is perceptible only through the eyes of faith. It is that light which, in the words of St. Gregory, "was hidden from the Jews, but shone forth to the heathen."[6]

On the left side of the cave, we see the magi. They represent, as I have already indicated, persons who must travel a great way from that which they can grasp by the intellect to that which every child senses by intuition. They represent the experience of conversion which for many is neither a pleasant experience nor one that is sudden and banishes all doubt. T.S. Eliot, in his poem *Journey of the Magi,* describes conversion as he knew it to a slow, painful process. In the poem, the old magus who is narrator is Eliot himself:

> Were we led all that way for Birth or Death? There was a Birth, certainly, we had evidence and no doubt. I had seen birth and death, but had thought they were different; this birth was hard and bitter agony for us, like Death, our Death.[7]

In the icon, the magi are depicted as being of different ages, which indicates that revelation comes independently of age, wisdom and experience.[8] In some icons, the magi represent the different races of humankind, fulfilling by their presence the words of Isaiah:

> The Lord shall rise above you
> and his glory surround you,
> nations shall come towards your light
> and kings to your brightness (Isaiah 60:3).

If the shepherds represent believing Israel, the magi represent believing pagans.

Another detail bears mention which — although it is apocryphal — is surely appropriate. In the bottom right hand corner we see the midwives whose role it is to deal with the consequences of human birth. They provide a necessary corrective to the heretical notion that Christ only appeared to be human. Here he is seen being bathed as any human baby. In nearly every representation, these women appear with bare arms. There is a legend which says that when Joseph hired them to help with the baby, they laughed when he told them that this was the Son of God. As a consequence of their unbelief, their arms withered on the spot. But as they bathed the babe, their withered limbs became whole again. This indicates that paralysis is antecedent to faith, and that wholeness returns when faith appears.

The cave is a symbol of death in other icons, and that is certainly the case here. But here, the cave is also earth's gift to the Child, which shelters the Sun of Life in the midst of the shadow of death.[9]

The manger is also earth's gift to the Child, but in this case the 'earth' is seen as the wilderness. This affords a comparison between the manna produced by the desert of the Exodus, and the Bread of Life which comes to birth in this desert place. The desert motif stands for the rejection of the world, for it is an empty, uninhabited place. It stands in stark contrast to the world of men and women. This motif recalls the words of John's Gospel:

> He was in the world
> and the world was made by him;
> he came to his own home
> but his own people did not take him in
> (John 1:10-11).

The manger here is no ordinary hay trough but a tiny sepulchre, and the swaddling clothes prefigure the babe's burial shroud. This brings us up short, and forces us to link the Incarnation with Resurrection. Eliot's old magus utters the truth, "I had seen birth and death but had thought they were different.."

The presence of the ox and the ass is no mere bucolic detail. They indicate that the whole animal world recognizes the Incarnation of the Son of God. He is their Savior too. Their presence also fulfills the prophecy of Isaiah:

> The ox knows its owner
> and the ass his owner's manger
> but Israel knows nothing,
> my own people have no understanding
> (Isaiah 1:3).

In the center of the icon is the Virgin Mother. She is the fixed point around which everything revolves. The Orthodox believe her to be humankind's highest thanksgiving to God. Kallistos Ware summarizes the intent of her place in the composition: "From this it can be seen how high a place of honour we Orthodox ascribe to the Holy Virgin in our theology and prayer. She is for us the supreme offering made by the human race to God."[10]

The Orthodox venerate Mary as the new Eve. Just as the first Eve became "the mother of all those who live" (Genesis 3:20), the Virgin Mother of God becomes the mother of a new humanity, raised and deified through the Incarnation of

45

her Son.[11] Although she rests next to the Child, it is no accident that she reclines outside the cave. She is the firstborn of a new humanity, raised by her obedience to perfect life.

When I first began to paint icons, I was troubled by the incidental position Joseph occupies. He is always situated in a corner, quite distant from the events that unfold in the icon. His expression clearly indicates that he cannot comprehend the wonder of the event. He represents righteous Israel, and knows that he is entitled — even obligated by Jewish Law — to divorce his new wife on the grounds of adultery. The devil, disguised as an old shepherd, stands before him, tempting him to unbelief. The face of the Virgin, distant yet comprehending his pain, is turned toward him. Her gaze is one of compassion — a symbol for those beset by doubts and difficulties in believing.[12]

When I began to paint my first icon of the Nativity, I was determined to place Joseph by Mary's side. My intent was to demonstrate that the "fathering" role is as important as the "mothering" role. I was as yet unable to separate "fathering" from simple biology. My parishoners approved of the prominence I gave Joseph, but our Greek neighbors were horrified. Another Orthodox lady volunteered, "This is a nice religious painting, but it is *not* an icon!" I asked my mentor to explain what she had meant and he replied, "If you're going to be an iconographer, you simply cannot compromise the mystery of the Incarnation. An apocryphal detail such as the presence of the midwives, may be added, but you simply cannot take away that which is essential. The reason your Nativity is not an icon is precisely because it is *your* Nativity."

The icon of the Nativity tells us that the mystery of the Incarnation is exactly *that* — a Mystery. Like the magi, if we are going to find the Child, we may have to cast aside our common sense as well as the misgivings that come of learning. This struggle — this search — we find reflected in that great Charles Wesley hymn "Love Divine, All Love Excelling." This hymn, like the "Glory to God" reprised by the shepherds, is appropriate for the likes of the magi, who at last kneel before the Child:

Finish then thy new creation;
Pure and spotless let us be.
Let us see the great salvation
Perfectly restored in thee
Changed from glory into glory,
Till in heaven we take our place,
Till we cast our crowns before thee,
Lost in wonder, love and praise.[13]

1   *Byzantine Daily Worship,* Alleluia Press, PO Box 103, Allendale NJ., 07401. 1969., p. 571. Kontakion (Third Tone) Feast of the Nativity.
2   Ouspensky, Leonid and Lossky, Vladimir, *The Meaning of Icons,* St. Vladimir's Seminary Press, Crestwood, NY., 10707., 1982., p. 157
3   Ibid., p. 157.
4   Op. Cit., pp. 560-561.
5   Op. Cit., p. 159.
6   As cited by Ouspensky and Lossky., p. 159.
7   Eliot, T.S., *Collected Poems,* Harcourt, Brace & World., 1963.
8   Op. Cit., p. 159.
9   From a homily attributed to Gregory of Nyssa, as cited by Ouspensky and Lossky., p. 157.
10 Ware, Kallistos, *The Orthodox Way.,* St. Vladimir's Seminary Press, Crestwood, NY., 10707., 1980., p. 103.
11 Op. Cit., p. 159.
12 Baggley, John, *Doors of Perception — Icons and Their Spiritual Significance,* St. Vladimir's Seminary Press., Crestwood, NY., 10707., p. 142.
13 *The Methodist Hymnal,* The Methodist Publishing House, Nashville, TN., 1964., #283.

THE PRESENTATION

Simeon, receive now the One whom Moses the
Lawgiver had foreseen through the cloud on Sinai,
becoming a Child and submitting Himself to the
Law, He whom the Law had described and the
prophets foretold. O Lord who for our sake were
incarnate and saved mankind, to You we bow in
worship![1]

Every ritual and ceremony begins as an effort to bridge
the gulf between the human and the divine. There comes a
time, however, when these forms restrict rather than help
the movement of the Spirit of God. When the *form* of worship becomes the *object* of worship, then the Spirit must
seek expression in some new and living way. One might say
that the "new and living way" is made manifest in the icon
of the Presentation of Christ.

Luke reveals in chapter 2:21-40 that Mary and Joseph
were very much part of the Old Covenant and participated
in all of its forms, even at great hardship and sacrifice.

Since ancient times, firstborn males had been believed to
be the property of God. Since the priestly tribe of Levi had
been set apart in their stead, the firstborn of other tribes
could be "redeemed" through payment of a nominal
redemption price to the priest (Numbers 8:15 ff.). Exodus
13:2 had laid down, "Consecrate every first-born to me, the
first of every womb among the sons of Israel. Whether man
or beast, it is mine."

This is one of the reasons why Mary and Joseph appeared in the Temple — to "redeem" their firstborn son.

The other reason was so that Mary could perform the rite
of purification which was to occur forty days after the birth
of a male child (Leviticus 12:6-8).

In Luke's telling, the theme of purification is almost
forgotten. Nor does he develop the idea of "redemption"

(Exodus 13:13). He interprets Jesus' presentation in light of the Old Testament story about Samuel, dedicated by his mother to the service of God (I Samuel 1:24-28).

The Orthodox East perceives in this event the Spirit's breaking out of old forms, thus revealing the Word in a new and living way. It becomes a meeting of the Old and New Covenants, which is why the Feast of the Presentation, and the icon that depicts the event, is called "The Meeting of Our Lord and Savior Jesus Christ."[2] At this meeting it is revealed that the Savior comes as a light to the pagans, and thus a light of revelation to the whole world.

It was not the will of the Father that Israel should keep the treasure of the Covenant for herself; her glory was intended to be in making all her life a light to the world. Salvation, says the Evangelist, "..comes from the Jews" (John 4:22), but this salvation, says Paul, is "..the power of God saving all who have faith — the Jews first, but the Greeks as well" (Romans 1:16).

In additon to the theme of "meeting", the icon portrays two underlying motifs: the gesture of offering, symbolized by Mary and Joseph with their hands raised; and prophecy — Simeon and Anna being representatives of the prophetic strain within faithful Israel.

The gesture of offering includes the element of sacrifice required for ritual purification under the Law, but it is primarily the offering of the Incarnate Son to Israel and the world.

The offering of Joseph is two doves, for "Such is the law concerning a woman who gives birth to either a boy or a girl. If she is not able to bring a lamb, she is to take two turtledoves or two young pigeons, one for the burnt offering and the other for the sacrifice of sin" (Leviticus 12:8).

In this it is implicitly stated that the Holy family was desperately poor in addition to being devout. The Eastern Church, in a poignant interpretation of this gesture, includes a hymn within the liturgy of the Presentation which says that the two doves indicate that Christ is head of both the

Old Covenant and the New.[3] This, I submit, is an example of how the Holy Spirit works to invigorate an old symbol by investing it with new meaning.

Mary's offering is twofold. The Mother of God is offering herself for purification, but this is eclipsed by that other offering which is her Son. As she hands the babe to Simeon we are reminded of Abraham's near sacrifice of Isaac. This point is underscored by the fact that Simeon holds the Child over the altar of sacrifice. The Mother of God is offering the Son to all who will receive him with gladness, but she is also offering him to those who will mock him and crucify him. The Child seems to know instinctively what is ahead. He reaches for his mother who draws back as though instinctively she too knows what lies ahead.

Simeon's message is addressed to her only, and not to Joseph. In this it is revealed that only Mary will live long enough to witness this sacrifice and that she will suffer bitterly in its course. It is through those who suffer that other souls receive life's meaning. Her purification will be through suffering and this will be her glory. Hers will be Unamuno's ironic blessing, "May God deny you peace and give you glory."[4]

Simeon, as I have already indicated, is a representative of the Old Covenant. He and John the Baptist will be the last in that prophetic strain inspired by the Spirit to declare God's Holy Word to Israel. Some interpreters have identified him with a rabbi of the First Century who was a son of Hillel and the father of Gamaliel (Acts 5:34; 22:3). His words may in fact be an early Christian hymn—a hymn which serves Luke's interest in stressing the universality of the Gospel:

> Now Lord, allow your servant to go in peace,
> just as you promised;
> because my eyes have seen the salvation
> which you have prepared before all the nations

a light for the gentiles
and the glory of your people Israel (Luke
2:29-32).

Luke stresses here that Israel's prophetic tradition itself recognized the Christ even as a babe in arms, and that the salvation he brings was intended for all humankind. Such news is so astonishing that even the holy family is caught off its guard. God has ordained that the Child should separate the righteous from the unrighteous among many in Israel! Some will reject him and fall (Isaiah 8:14-15). Others will accept him and rise. He will be a sign (Luke 11:30) that many will dispute. But this is part of the purpose of God, for by their attitude toward Christ, men and women will reveal their true nature.

Anna too is a representative of the Old Covenant. Her presence is significant if only for the fact that women in the ancient world were deemed insignificant. Her presence anticipates the New Covenant where, as Paul says in Galatians 3:28: "..there are no more distinctions between Jew and Greek, slave and free, male and female, but all of you are one in Christ Jesus..."

In calling her a prophetess, Luke is according her a recognition rare in Hebrew history. Only seven prophetesses had prophesied to Israel: Sarah, Miriam, Deborah, Hannah, Abigail, Huldah and Esther. Possibly Anna belonged to an order of widows with specifically religious functions in the Temple. It is not certain from the Greek text whether we are to understand that she was eighty-four years of age, or had been a widow for that length of time. She symbolizes patience, waiting and longing—a true Israelite. She will announce the redemption of Israel to all who await it. Not many, however, will be looking for this kind of redemption.

Alexander Solzhenitsyn may have had Anna in mind in his short story, *Matryona's House.* The proverbial babushka, Matryona was:

misunderstood and rejected by her husband, a stranger to her own family despite her happy, amiable temperament, comical, so foolish that she worked for others for no reward, this woman, who had buried all her six children, had stored up no earthly goods. Nothing but a dirty white goat, a lame cat, and a row of fig plants.

None of us who lived close to her perceived that she was that one righteous person, without whom, as the saying goes, no city can stand.

Neither can the whole world.[5]

The icon of the Presentation tells us in a quiet, serene way that God is the ultimate iconoclast — the One who smashes our dearest idols, and bypasses our most pious hopes in order that we might know that we have no claim on Him. All of Israel's preparation had not prepared her for this kind of God. He becomes the suffering Messiah who concentrates all her holy laws into a single commandment. His is the Spirit who — one way or another — will see to it that her worship and hope becomes universalized.

The architectural setting of the icon recalls the Temple with its altar and canopy. It represents the institutional Church also. It reminds us that all institutions which claim divine sanction will remain only so far as they remain faithful to the Divine Will.

The setting also serves as a device to draw the spectator into the activity going on within the enclosure which becomes a paradigm for the human soul. Thus, if we are willing, we ourselves become participants in the icon. We become faithful Simeon with arms outstretched. We become patient, faithful Anna. The Mother of God offers her Son to us. Will we receive him gladly, or mock him and crucify him? Joseph shows us the poverty of his sacrifice, which, like the widow's mite, is effective out of all proportion to its value. It tells us that the Old Covenant is fulfilled in the New and that Christ is the Lord of both. It tells us also that entry into the Covenant relationship requires sacrifice.

An appropriate restating of the message of Luke 2:21-40 and the icon of the Presentation is contained in the last verse of Richard Crashaw's mystical poem *The Nativity of Our Lord God:*

> To thee, meek majesty! soft king
> of simple graces and sweet loves!
> Each of us his lamb will bring.
> Each his pair of silver doves!
> Till burnt at last in the fire of Thy fair eyes,
> Ourselves become our own best sacrifice.[6]

---

1   *Byzantine Daily Worship,* Alleluia Press, PO Box 103, Allendale NJ., 07401. 1969., p. 627. Kontakion (First Tone, 3 and 4).

2   Baggley, John, *Doors of Perception — Icons and Their Spiritual Significance,* St. Vladimir's Seminary Press., Crestwood, NY., 10707., 1988., p. 126

3   Op. Cit., p. 629.

4   Unamuno, Miguel de, *The Tragic Sense of Life in Man and in Peoples,* Macmillan Co., NY., 1921. (Tr. J.E. Crawford Flitch).

5   Solzhenitsyn, Alexander, *Stories and Prose Poems,* Farrar, Straus and Giroux., NY., 1970., p. 52.

6   Miles Hill, Caroline, *The World's Greatest Religious Poetry,* Macmillan Co., NY., 1923., p. 321.

THE BAPTISM OF OUR LORD

O, our Savior, the armies of angels trembled when
they saw You baptized by your servant and the
Holy Spirit bearing witness by coming down, and
when they heard the Father's voice speaking from
heaven: 'This One upon whom the Forerunner
lays his hands is my beloved Son in whom I am
well pleased.' O Christ God, glory to You![1]

The Orthodox refer to the Baptism of our Lord as
Epiphany, or "manifestation," because at his baptism, our
Lord was first revealed to the people. The feast is also called
the Theophany, or the "manifestation of God," because
thereby — as the icon reveals — the Trinity was first revealed
to the world of the senses.

In the upper part of the icon we see the heavenly sphere
which penetrates the earthly realm. From this sphere, above
the Savior's head, a ray descends, revealing the form of a
dove. Thus we have — albeit indirectly — a depiction of the
Father, Son and Holy Spirit.

The difficulty of depicting the torso of our Lord while
fully covered with water is one that has always defied solu-
tion. In the icon he is shown standing against a background
of water, as though in a cave. Once again, the cave is symbolic of the abyss, or of death and burial. This device serves
to emphasize the humility of the one who empties himself
(Philippians 2:7) taking on the form of a servant, becoming
subject to death with the whole creation.[2]

While this representation shows Christ covered with a
loincloth the majority of older icons show him naked, in
that the Incarnation brings with it the possibility of the
restoration of humankind to its lost innocence. As the
liturgy of the feast expresses it:

And you, Adam, rejoice with the first Mother, Eve,
and hide not as you did of old in paradise: for

61

Christ at the sight of you naked has come forth to
clothe you with the robe of innocence. Indeed,
Christ has come to renew the whole creation.[3]

Our Lord is depicted reaching with his right hand
toward the Baptizer, indication that the initiative is his own:
the Master comes to the servant to be baptized. At the same
time, he blesses the waters of the Jordan, the waters of
chaos, so that they may become for the Church the means
of new birth into the life of Christ.

The Baptizer places his right hand on our Lord's head in
an ancient baptismal gesture, while lifting his left hand in a
gesture of prayer.

The presence of angels may puzzle Protestants as they
are not mentioned in scripture as being present at the event.
They serve to remind us that the whole cosmos, the visible
as well as the invisible realm, bows in wonderment before
the Son. The angels cover their hands with their cloaks in an
ancient gesture of reverence. Or, are they playing the role of
attendants, waiting to cover their Lord's body as he emerges
from the depths?

In Baptism, as at Passover, our Lord is raising an old
ritual to new life. The Jews were familiar with ritual
washings, as five chapters of the book of Leviticus attest
(11-15). Symbolic washing and purifying were woven into
the fabric of Jewish life.

Gentiles, who did not observe any part of Jewish ritual,
were regarded by the Jews as ceremonially unclean. During
the time of Jesus, any gentile who wished to become part of
the covenant would be received only after three ceremonies
were performed: circumcision — for this was a mark of the
Covenant people; sacrifice — made on his or her behalf
because of the need for atonement through the shedding of
blood; and baptism — for cleansing from all the pollutions
incurred through his or her past life.

The baptism of John the Baptist was different from
anything that had gone before, because John was asking

Jews to submit to that which only a gentile was supposed to need. Thus it is revealed that it is not the Jewish life, but the cleansed life that matters to God. Jesus received this baptism so that we, who desire to become part of this new creation, might do likewise.

Baptism into the Christian faith must be accompanied by confession. Without humiliation, and the confession that follows it, there can be no forgiveness, and hence no "turning" to God.

Anthony Bloom has this to say about the humility that must precede confession:

> Basically, humility is the attitude of one who stands constantly under the judgment of God. It is the attitude of one who is like the soil. Humility comes from the Latin word *humus*, fertile ground. The fertile ground is there, unnoticed, taken for granted, always there to be trodden upon. It is silent, inconspicuous, dark and yet it is always ready to receive any seed, ready to give it substance and life. The more lowly, the more fruitful, because it becomes really more fertile when it accepts all the refuse of the earth. It is so low that nothing can spoil it, abase it, humiliate it; it has accepted the last place and cannot go any lower. In that position nothing can shatter the soul's serenity, its peace and joy.[4]

Confession, if it is to precede a change of mind, a new direction of the will, and an altered purpose in life, must be threefold. One must confess to himself or herself! One must then make confession to those whom he or she has wronged. Most important, one must make confession to God.

We find a model for confession to one's self in Luke's telling of the parable of the prodigal son. The prodigal "came to himself." He clearly saw his predicament as the result of self-destructive behavior. He realized that he had no chance of extricating himself from his pitiful state, so he returned to his father and begged for a place in his house, if only as a hired servant. William Barclay has this to say about confession to one's self:

> Someone tells of a man's first step to grace. As he was shaving one morning he looked at his face in the mirror and suddenly said, 'You dirty little rat!' And from that day he was a changed man.[5]

A person must make confession to those whom he or she has wronged. Confession to another — especially the person one has harmed — is crucial to the Alcoholics Anonymous' twelve-step program for recovery. Step eight says "(we) made a list of all the persons we had harmed, and became willing to make amends to them all." Step nine continues, "We made direct amends to such people wherever possible, except when to do so would injure them or others."[6] Human barriers have to be removed before we can approach God (Matthew 5:23-24).

Finally, one must make confession to God. This must be a more or less continuous process because, although conversion begins in us, it never ends. Bloom indicates that it must be an "increasing process in which we gradually become more and more what we should be until, after the day of judgment, these categories of fall and righteousness disappear and are replaced by new categories of a new life. As Christ says, 'I make all things new.'"[7]

From Nineteenth Century Russia comes the little book, *The Way of the Pilgrim.* It is the story of the life of a peasant who heard read a portion of the First Epistle to the Thessalonians where it says, "Pray without ceasing (5;15)." He wandered from Church to Church to try to discover how it was possible to pray without ceasing, till finally he came upon a holy man who taught him a simple prayer called the Jesus Prayer: "Lord Jesus Christ, Son of God, have mercy upon me, a sinner." The peasant repeated the prayer thousands of times with his lips until finally the prayer, by its own action, passed from his lips to his heart. He says, "..it seemed as though my heart in its ordinary beating began to say the prayer with each beat...I gave up saying the prayer with my lips. I simply listened carefully to what my heart was saying."[8]

Confessional prayer is effective only as it is continually lived-out in life. Unless life and prayer become one, prayer becomes, according to Bloom, a sort of polite madrigal which we offer to God at moments when we are giving time to him.[9]

The way of confessional prayer is like the way of the cross related in Mark's Gospel:

> If anyone wants to be my follower, let him deny himself and take up his cross and follow me. For anyone who wants to save his live will lose it; but anyone who loses his life for my sake, and for the sake of the Gospel, will save it (8:34).

The relationship of conversion to which baptism is the door, purges arrogance, self-righteousness and self-pity. It brings hope, a nobler vision, and a deeper serenity.

We see in Jesus' baptism the infinite compassion of God.

> To us, who cry out from the depths of our brokenness for a hand that will touch us, an arm that can embace us, lips that will kiss us, a word that speaks to us here and now, and a heart that is not afraid of our fears and tremblings; to us who feel our pain as no other human being feels it, has felt it or will ever feel it and who are always waiting for someone who dares to come close — to us a man has come who could truly say, 'I am with you.'[10]

If we would join Christ in his Baptism we must discover, as Henri Nouwen puts it, that "nothing human is alien to us..the roots of all conflict, war, injustice, cruelty, hatred, jealousy and envy are deeply anchored in our own heart."[11]

We must die to our neighbors. This seems to say that we must stop judging them and stop evaluating them. Judgements create a distance between us and them, and where there is a distance, we cannot really *be* with others.[12]

The gentle, forgiving person is so deeply convinced of sin as to be more fully aware of God's great mercy. This is what it means to be "filled with the presence of God."[13]

When we are filled with God's merciful presence we can do nothing other than minister, because our whole being reflects the light of the Incarnation — a light that has come among us to shine in our darkness.

[1] *Byzantine Daily Worship,* Alleluia Press, PO Box 103, Allendale NJ., 07401. 1969., p. 592. Vespers, Feast of the Theophany of Our Lord, God and Saviour Jesus Christ.

[2] Baggley, John, *Doors of Perception — Icons and Their Spiritual Significance,* St. Vladimir's Seminary Press, Crestwood, NY., 10707., 1988., p. 124.

[3] Op. Cit., p. 587., Troparion of the Preparation.

[4] Bloom, Anthony, *Living Prayer,* Templegate Publishers, Springfield, IL., 1966., p. 98.

[5] Barclay, William, *The Gospel of Mark,* Westminster Press., Philadelphia., PA., 1975., p. 14.

[6] *Alcoholics Anonymous,* Alcoholics Anonymous World Services, Inc., NY., 1976., p. 59.

[7] Op. Cit., Bloom., p. 66.

[8] French, R.M., (Translator), *The Way of the Pilgrim,* Seabury Press., NY., 1965., pps. 19-20.

[9] Op. Cit., Bloom., p. 59.

[10] McNeill, Donald P., Morrison, Douglas A., and Nouwen, Henri, J.M., *Compassion: A Reflection on the Christian Life.,* Doubleday & Company., NY., 1983., p. 23.

[11] Nouwen, Henri J.M., *The Way of the Heart,* Ballantine Books, 201 E. 50th. St., New York, NY., 1981., p. 20.

[12] Ibid., p. 21.

[13] Ibid., p. 22.

THE TRANSFIGURATION OF OUR LORD

O Lord, when You were transfigured on a high mountain in the presence of your foremost disciples, You radiated with glory, showing how those who lead an outstanding life of virtue will be made worthy of the glory of heaven. Elias and Moses, conversing with the Lord, showed Him to be the Lord of the Living and the Dead, God who spoke through the Law and the Prophets — the same to whom the Father's voice bore witness out of the bright cloud, saying: 'Hear him, for it is he, through his cross, who despoiled Hades and granted eternal life to the dead.'[1]

The Greek Fathers describe the encounter with God as like our walking up a mist-covered mountain. We take a step forward and suddenly we are on the edge of a precipice and discover to our alarm that there is no solid ground beneath our feet, but only the bottomless abyss. It is like standing at night in a darkened room. We open the blinds and suddenly there is a flash of lightning which causes us to stagger backwards in momentary blindness. When we come face to face with the mystery of God, all the familiar footholds vanish, and there seems to be nothing to which we can cling.[2]

Because God is a mystery, wholly Other, and beyond understanding, we must — if we would seek the divine — be prepared to believe that there are times, places and events in which the divine extends to us the possibility of seeing. God does, I believe, provide us with moments of eternity in time. When these moments occur, we are able to perceive the energy of God according to our need and our willingness to continue our journey.

Kallistos Ware puts it this way:

To be a Christian is to be a traveler. Our situation..is like that of the Israelite people in the desert of Sinai: we live in tents, not houses, for spiritually we are always on the move. We are on a journey not measured by the hours of our watch or the days of the calendar, for it is a journey out of time and into eternity.[3]

The Transfiguration was for Jesus and the disciples one of these moments of eternity in time. It occurred in the midst of a crisis for the disciples and for Jesus. The disciples' journey had not yet revealed the type of Messiah that Jesus would be. Peter's confession at Caesarea Philippi that Jesus was the Christ earned him a rebuke from Jesus when he refused to hear that the Messiah would die. For Jesus, Peter's confession was a little Gethsemane, a look into a future almost too painful to contemplate. The Transfiguration would become for Jesus and the disciples the kind of moment we often receive when discouragement has taken its frightful toll and we find that we do not have the spiritual energy and resources to press on. Looking back, we sometimes wonder how it was that this moment occurred, seemingly in the nick of time, forestalling disaster, and putting us back on the right path. Well might we wonder where we would be, had not this moment — this means of grace — occurred.

The Transfiguration took place on a high mountain. In the presence of the disciples Peter, James and John, Jesus became radiant with an unearthly light and his clothes appeared dazzling white. Then there appeared Moses and Elijah talking to him. Next a cloud came, covering them in shadow and they heard a voice from the cloud saying, "This is my Son, the Beloved. Listen to him." Then, looking around, the disciples discovered that Jesus was alone.

Ware continues:

Although non-physical, the divine light can be seen..through physical eyes, provided that the

72

senses have been transformed by divine grace. Our eyes do not behold the light through natural powers of perception, but through the power of the Holy Spirit acting within him.[4]

As a means of grace, the Transfiguration is a "mysterious signpost to the future of God."[5] This is no less true for the Church than it was for the disciples and for Jesus.

For Jesus, the Transfiguration was a mighty confirmation of his vision of Messiahship. As before, at his baptism, the Father testified from heaven, "This is my Son, the Beloved.." (Mark 9:8). Here again the Spirit descends, but as a cloud of light.[6]

The appearance of Moses and Elijah is accounted for by John Chrysostom. Both had received a secret vision of God — Moses on Mt. Sinai and Elijah on Mt. Carmel. Moses represents the dead, while Elijah, taken up to heaven on a chariot of fire, represents the living. More significantly, Moses represents the Law, and Elijah represents the Prophets.[7] William Barclay, commenting on the appearance of these personages, says, "When the greatest of the law-givers and the greatest of the prophets met with Jesus, it was to say, 'Go on!' "[8] This visitation indicated to Jesus that his passion, death and resurrection would be the culmination of the whole of prophetic tradition and the Law, and that Moses and the Prophets had looked forward to his coming with great longing.

At the moment of his deepest humiliation on the cross, this vision of glorification would give him strength. For, as we ourselves know, almost any agony can be borne if it is for some purpose. Conversely, any agony that seems pointless and arbitrary leads us quickly to defeat.

The Transfiguration was for the disciples a means of grace. They had been shattered by Jesus' statement at Caesarea Philippi that he was going to Jerusalem to be killed. That seemed a complete denial of everything for which they had hoped and dreamed about the Messiah and his kingdom.[9] After the Transfiguration, they would be able to perceive Jesus' passion as the beginning of God's Kingdom, coming in power. Looking back on the cross of Christ, they would see not only a suffering man, but suffering God.[10] They would look toward his appearing at the Second Coming, and coming in glory upon the occasions of their own martyrdoms.

John, for his part, would pass the vision along to his disciples who would remember his words, "God is light and in him is no darkness at all" (I John 1:15).

Peter's disciples would preserve his recollection of the event:

> It was not any artfully devised fables that we were repeating when we brought you the knowledge of the power and the coming of our Lord Jesus Christ; we ourselves were eyewitnesses of his majesty. He received honor and glory from the Father, when the sublime glory itself spoke to him and said, 'This is my Son the Beloved, in whom I am well pleased.' We ourselves heard this, spoken from heaven, when we were with him on the holy mountain (II Peter 1:16-18).

The Transfiguration is a means of grace for the Church, because it affords us a glimpse of life after the resurrection. It tells us that the resurrected body will resemble the body we have now, but it will be transformed. St. Cyril says, "It is the selfsame body that is raised, although not in its present state of weakness, for it will 'put on incorruption.' "[11]

The Transfiguration shows us that in the Kingdom of God each one is with the others, yet distinctly himself or herself, bearing the same characteristics as in this life, but with these healed, renewed and glorified.[12]

The Transfiguration tells us that our faith journey survives death. This is what Paul means when he says that we will continue to go forward, growing "brighter as we are transformed into the image that we reflect" (II Corinthians

3:18). God always has something more to teach us, and we always have something more to learn of him."[13]

Set within Glacier Park in the Rocky Mountains is St. Mary's Lake. It is a scene of indescribable beauty. On the shore there used to be a raised platform. A sign identified the spot as a "postcard view." On sunny days, the line of visitors to the platform was often several hundred feet long. It was reported that many people joined the line without really knowing why, and that when they arrived at the platform they took pictures of the sign without ever pausing to look at the view. This, I fear, may describe our faith journey. We wait in line for a sign, and when it is before us, we miss the vision because the grandeur is just too perplexing — too unsettling — for us to receive with joy.

It is not the function of the Christian faith to provide easy answers to our every question, but to nudge us little by little until the "sign" is before us. God, Ware suggests, "is not so much the object of our knowledge as the cause of our wonder."[14] Unless we begin the journey with a receptivity to awe and astonishment, we shall miss those moments of eternity in time that God sets before us. Consequently, we will make little progress on the way.

[1]   *Byzantine Daily Worship,* Alleluia Press, PO Box 103, Allendale, NJ., 07401. 1969., pps. 746-747. Vespers, Feast of the Transfiguration.
[2]   Ware, Kallistos, *The Orthodox Way,* St. Vladimir's Seminary Press., Crestwood, NY., 10707., 1980., p. 15.
[3]   Ibid., p. 8.
[4]   Ibid., p. 171.
[5]   Berkhof, Hendrikus, *Well-Founded Hope,* John Knox Press., Richmond, VA., 1969., p. 35.
[6]   Ouspensky, Leonid and Lossky, Vladimir, *The Meaning of Icons,* St. Vladimir's Seminary Press., Crestwood, NY., 10707., p. 212.
[7]   Barclay, William, *The Gospel of Mark,* Westminster Press, Philadelphia., PA., 1975., p. 211.
[8]   Ibid., p. 211.
[9]   Op. Cit., Ouspensky., p. 211.
[10] Op. Cit., Ware., p. 106.
[11] Ibid., p. 182.
[12] Ibid., p. 184.
[13] Ibid., p. 185.
[14] Ibid., p. 16.

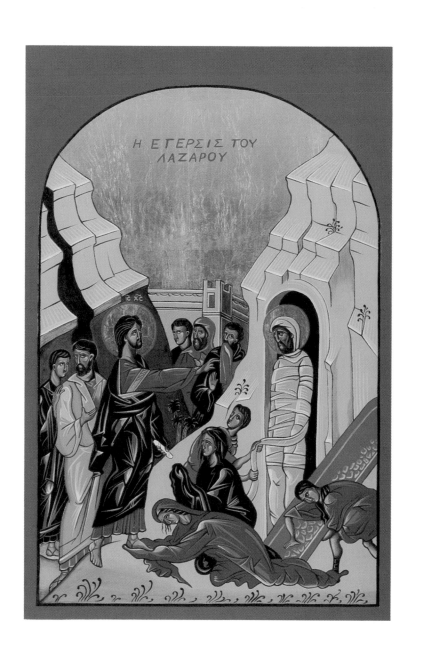

THE RAISING OF LAZARUS

O Christ God, when You raised Lazarus from the dead, before the time of your passion, You confirmed the future resurrection of all. We too, like the children of old, carry before You the symbols of your triumph and victory and cry out to You, the Conqueror of Death: 'Hosanna in the Highest! Blessed is He who comes in the name of the Lord!'[1]

Travelers to the holy land report that a scant two miles from Jerusalem there is a village named El Azariyeh. It is an Arabic name and it means *Lazarus*.[2] When its name was changed from Bethany I do not know, but it has not been in the recent past. We learn from Raymond Brown that an ossuary was recently found in the vicinity, inscribed with the names of Mary, Martha, and Lazarus.[3] While we know full well that many places in that part of the world which purport to be the resting place of a saint are in fact the product of fantasy or wishful thinking, our skepticism is brought up short in this case. For, if John's Gospel is to be believed, we must acknowledge that something quite extraordinary happened at El Azariyeh — something that has never been forgotten.

If John's chronology is correct, this "something" ignited a frenzy on the day we call Palm Sunday, causing Caiaphas and his crew to plot an ugly little show-trial and a "hurry-up" execution. One does not raise the dead in the presence of a company of mourners and expect everyone to forget all about it. This is what happened at El Azariyeh, and John uses the telling of this event to highlight two of his favorite themes — "glorification," and "light and life." He also includes the central theme of the Church that Jesus Christ *is* the resurrection and the life.

A few words about "glorification" may be in order, because what Jesus meant by it, and what we and the disciples mean by it, are poles apart. To us, glorification may mean something like winning the Academy Award, the Nobel Prize, or — if we happen to be clergy — getting the nod from the bishop to move up the "ladder." We know that the first disciples were one with us because of the way they jostled one another for the best seats in the Kingdom.

They did not know — could not know — that for Jesus, glorification and crucifixion were of a piece. When Jesus first received word that Lazarus was ill and said that his sickness would not end in death but would glorify God, they must have assumed that he was talking nonsense. They knew only that if Jesus went anywhere in the vicinity of Jerusalem, he was as good as dead himself. What would be the glory in that?

Later they would understand that we are bound for participation in a completely renewed and infinitely exalted form of human existence — bound for glory as it were. But then they were still too world-bound to see anything but those things the world regards as glorious. Later they would say much about glory, and about reflecting the divine nature. Even Peter would write that in Christ we become partakers of the divine nature (2 Peter 1:4). But as yet they were too ambitious for themselves to reflect much of the divine image.

They would learn that Jesus' glorification went straight through the cross, and this still holds true for the Church and our unsaved world.

Only through a deep transformation do we become suited for a world in which God will be all in all. If anonymity becomes our lot, or loss of self-esteem, or powerlessness, it makes all the difference in the world if we see our state as the means of our glorification and our way to God.

The second of John's themes is light and life. They are as inseparably joined here as in the opening verses of the Gospel — verses which proclaim, "In him was life, and that life was the light of men (1:4)." This theme is restated at the tomb of Lazarus in what we take as an aside comment overheard in the general murmuring of the spectators, "He opened the eyes of the blind man; could he not have prevented this man's death?"

John realized that the blind man and the dead man Lazarus served as signs to the unbelieving world. Jesus used these healings to reveal himself as the "enfleshment" of the same divine Word that brings light and life to creation. Jesus' healing of the blind man showed that in him was light, and the raising of Lazarus that in him was life. Whoever would receive the gifts of light and life through belief in him would never die a spiritual death, for this light and life leads to Eternal Life.

Even in our present state, belief in him causes our dead souls to rise out of the sleep of death, become alive, grow sensitive, active, purposeful, and become endowed with powers we did not have before. The Ephesian writer talks about this present "rebirth" as a type of resurrection: And you were dead, through the crimes and the sins in which you used to live when you were following the way of this world, obeying the ruler who governs the air, the spirit who is at work in the rebellious. We were all among them too in the past, living sensual lives, ruled entirely by our own physical desires and our own ideas; so that by nature we were as much under God's anger as the rest of the world. But God loved us with so much love that he was generous with his mercy: when we were dead through our sins, he brought us to life with Christ — it is through grace that you have been saved — and raised us up with him and gave us a place with him in heaven, in Jesus Christ (Eph. 2:1-6).

The third of John's themes is also the central claim of the Church. This John states in Jesus' poignant reassurance to Martha:

I am the resurrection. And no one who lives and believes in me will ever die...(11:26)

81

But this is no sterile ritual statement such as we sometimes recite as if by rote. For at the tomb, John shows us the deep sorrow of Jesus in the presence of death. Three sign-acts follow which show us the enormity of Jesus' grief—not only for Lazarus, but for the world.

Verse 33 has Jesus asking where he might find Lazarus' grave "with a sigh that came straight from the heart." The Greek verb is confusing here in that it seems wildly inappropriate to the occasion. The verb John chooses is "shuddered"—*(enebrimesato)*—used in classical literature for the snorting of a horse.[4] This seems to express not so much deep anguish as an anguish mixed with rage. We too may have experienced rage in the midst of death, but somehow felt it inappropriate, as if God would detect it and mete out a worse affliction than the death itself. But John shows us that grief mixed with rage in the presence of death was experienced by the Savior himself and therefore it cannot be an unforgivable sin. John Chrysostom suggests that what we have here is the same emotion that came over Jesus in the Garden of Gethsemane, brought on by the imminence of his own death and rage toward the Satan-dominated world that made his death inevitable.[5]

Verse 34—perhaps the most remembered in the New Testament—is "Jesus wept." To the gentile world this was a shocking thing, for if in Jesus we see revealed the image of God, then this is a strange sort of God indeed. Greek philosophy saw the primary characteristic of the gods as *apatheia*—the total inability to feel any emotion whatever.[6]

I used to wonder why Jesus did not simply pat the sisters on the head and say, "There, there, you two! Just wait and see! In a few moments you'll have your brother back safe and sound." We have all been afflicted with this sort of "comfort." Behind the condescending smile there often lurks an attitude which really means, "I really don't know the depth of your pain, and what is more, I'm not certain I really want to know!"

Jesus wept, not for Lazarus alone, but for the uncertainty, loneliness and pathos of life. "For it is not," writes the author of Hebrews, "as if we had a high priest who cannot sympathize with our weaknesses..(4:15)." I take from this that Christ is weeping still — weeping for the suffering that we face and must still face. I find in this a great comfort.

Verses 38-39 say, "Still sighing, Jesus reached the tomb (and) said, 'Take the stone away.' " If one can imagine him uttering this statement in a deep grief and rage, one can also imagine the alarm of the sisters who surely thought that he had gone mad. Was the shock of losing a brother to be intensified by digging him up again? Did he intend that they should face the stink and decomposition of a corpse four days dead?

The icon of the Raising of Lazarus may strike some of us as weird, but it intends to disturb us. It seeks to transmit the physical side of the miracle i.e., the external side. It seeks to make the event as accessible to us as it was to the eyewitnesses.[7]

Of course Lazarus would die again. When he came forth, the shrouds of death were still clinging to him. Contrast this scene with John's claim that Jesus' burial shroud lay there quite undisturbed. This tells us that our resurrection, rebirth in the here and now, is only the beginning of a process that will be completed in the Great Resurrection. Even the Holy Spirit is only a "guarantee" — no more than a firstfruits. Yet this resurrection in the here and now enables us to look forward with eager longing to the complete redemption of our existence.

Christ has already called us out of our existential pit of death, and will find our tomb and call us once more. Then we will leave the stink of death behind, put on the newness of the Resurrection, and sorrowing and sighing will be no more.

[1] *Byzantine Daily Worship,* Alleluia Press, PO Box 103, Allendale, NJ., 07401. 1969., p. 814. Saturday of Lazarus, Troparion (First Tone).

[2] Barclay, William, *The Gospel of John: Vol. II,* Westminster Press, Philadelphia., 1975., p. 102.

[3] Brown, Raymond, *The Anchor Bible: The Gospel According to John, I-XII,* Doubleday & Co., Garden City, NY., 1966., p. 431.

[4] Op. Cit., Barclay., p. 97.

[5] Op. Cit., Brown., p. 435.

[6] Op. Cit., Barclay., p. 98.

[7] Ouspensky, Leonid and Lossky, Vladimir, *The Meaning of Icons,* St. Vladimir's Seminary Press., Crestwood., NY., 10707., 1978., p. 175.

THE ENTRY

The Lord is God and He has appeared to us.
Therefore let us celebrate and sing for joy. Come,
let us glorify Christ and with palms and branches,
sing to Him canticles of praise: 'Hosanna! Blessed
is He who comes in the name of the Lord: Our
Saviour!'[1]

In the icon of The Entry, Christ rides sideways, his head
slightly turned to the apostles who are following behind, his
right hand blessing the crowd coming out of the city to meet
him.[2] In the icon, the city is all odd angles and of disjointed
perspective for this is no earthly city, but the heavenly
Jerusalem, where the laws of space and time are suspended.

There are children in the icon, cutting branches and
spreading garments in the Savior's way. Although no
Evangelist mentions their presence, Matthew does mention
the children who welcomed the Lord after his entry into
Jerusalem, when he drove the traders from the temple and
cured the sick.[3] Here are Jesus' own words remembered by
Matthew:

> Out of the mouths of infants and children you
> have brought praise (Matthew 21:16/Psalm 8:3).

Notice the people who come out of the city. Unlike the
children who welcome Jesus with joyful hearts, they appear
very grave. They are in a quandary, for they desperately
want a revolutionary leader, yet they are afraid of pushing
the tolerance of Rome too far. In a few days, when they
discover that Jesus is *not* what they expect, they will say to
Pilate, "Crucify him!"[4]

Although the religious authorities are a part of the
crowd, they see themselves as distinct from the crowd with

Jesus from Bethany, and the other crowd, rushing out of the city. They are convinced that what sets them apart is that they see the situation for what it really is, as John tells us from their meeting after the raising of Lazarus. This is what they had said:

> This man performs many signs and what are we doing about it? If we let him go on in this way everyone will believe in him and the Romans will come to destroy both our holy place and our nation (11:48-49)

In one sense, or so they reassured themselves, the demonstration would not amount to much. There were many in the throng who were simply sightseers, or in Jerusalem for the Passover; people simply caught up in the hysteria of the crowd. They were like many today who confuse "celebrity" with holiness, and follow this or that television evangelist. Holiness is a precious gift which cannot be received unless one desires nothing but Christ. Religious "personalities" who court celebrity ought to quake in their shoes once they have it, because the parade often becomes a howling mob!

In another sense, the authorities saw the demonstration as posing a grave danger, for here and there persons were shouting "Save now! Save now!" The authorities know the scriptures and were reminded of this portion of Psalm 118:

> Deliver us, Lord, deliver us.
> Grant us prosperity, Lord.
> Blessed is he who come in the name of the Lord.
> We bless you from the Lord's house.
> The Lord is God, his light shines in welcome.
> Bind the sacrifice with cords
> So that its boughs will reach
> As far as the horns of the altar..(Verses 25-27)

This same Psalm had been shouted by a crowd two hundred years earlier as Simon Maccabee rode into the city after taking the citadel from the hated Syrians. On that occasion, the inhabitants of Jerusalem had also waved palm branches because, "a great enemy had been crushed and thrown out of Israel" (I Maccabbees 13:51). The palm frond was and would remain a symbol of Jewish nationalism. It would appear again on the coins of the Second Revolt (AD 132-33).[5]

It is easy to see why the authorities, whose power was maintained by the Roman government, would view the situation with alarm.

John tells us that Jesus found a donkey and sat upon it only after the crowd had expressed its nationalistic expectations (John 12:14). Jesus realized that he could not reason with a mob, and so engaged himself in a prophetic action intended to counteract this nationalism. His action recalled the words of the prophet Zechariah:

> Be joyful, O daughter of Zion;
> cry out, O daughter of Jerusalem. Behold, your king
> comes to you: triumphant and victorious is he, humble
> and riding on an ass, on a colt, the foal of an ass.
> (Zechariah 9:9)

This action signified that Jesus was not the warrior figure of Israel's dreams, but the Prince of peace. For, as the next three verses attest:

> He will impose peace on the nations.
> His empire shall stretch from sea to sea,
> From the river to the ends of the earth (Zech. 9:10).

Jesus drew a dramatic picture of what he claimed to be, but no one understood his claim. Only the children seemed to understand. Their presence in the icon is reminiscent of Jesus' words in Matthew 18:3-4:

> I assure you that unless you change and become like little children again you shall not enter the kingdom of heaven. Whoever humbles himself like this little child is the greatest in the kingdom of heaven.

The Gospel lesson for Palm Sunday (John 12:12-16) ends with the irony of the Jewish authorities giving Jesus unwitting praise in their dismay: "You see, there is nothing you can do; look, the whole world is running after him (v. 19)." It is the world that the Savior redeems. John says in his third chapter:

> God so loved the world that he gave up his only-begotten Son, so that those who believe in him may not perish, but have eternal life (verse 16)

In the section of John's Gospel that follows Jesus' entry into Jerusalem, we are told of the Greeks who came to see Jesus. These were emissaries from this wider world which would soon begin to stir and respond.

Leonid Ouspensky, in his commentary on this icon, says of the religious authorities, "..they expect him to fulfill the prophecies by establishing the kingdom of Israel upon earth, that is, victory over enemies through their *physical annihilation.* Actually, the reverse is the case: victory over the enemies of Israel through their *spiritual salvation.*"[6]

Our idea of God tells us more about ourselves than about God. The saint has no desire for power over anyone, nor desire for victory over anyone, nor dominance over anyone because he or she knows only the mercy of God. The saint sees in Christ's entry into Jerusalem only this:

His scepter is his kindliness.
His grandeur is his grace.
His royalty is holiness
And love is in his face.[7]

Thomas Merton observes, "Do not think that you can show your love to Christ by hating those who seem to be his enemies on earth. Suppose they really do hate him: nevertheless he loves them and you cannot be united with him unless you love them too."[8]

John's vision embraces each one of us as a part of the transformed throng in the Resurrection — a throng that will carry palms and cry out in praise (Rev. 7:9). When we desire the Savior for himself, we praise him with childlike integrity. When we desire the Savior for himself, we may approach the image of God.

[1] *Byzantine Daily Worship,* Alleluia Press, PO Box 103., Allendale, NJ., 17401., 1969. p. 820. Hirmos (Fourth Tone).
[2] Ouspensky, Leonid and Lossky, Vladimir, *The Meaning of Icons,* St. Vladimir's Seminary Press, Crestwood, NY., 1982., pps. 176-177.
[3] Ibid., p. 177.
[4] Ibid., p. 178.
[5] Brown, Raymond, *The Gospel According to John I-XII.,* The Anchor Bible., Doubleday and Co., Garden City, NY., 1966., p. 460.
[6] Op. Cit., p. 178.
[7] *The Book of Hymns,* the United Methodist Publishing House, Nashville, TN., 1964., #422.
[8] Merton, Thomas, *New Seeds of Contemplation,* New Directions., p. 176.

THE CRUCIFIXION

> The cross is then the concrete expression of the
> Christian mystery, of victory by defeat, of glory
> by humiliation, of life by death — symbol of an
> omnipotent God, Who willed to become man and
> to die as a slave, in order to save his creature.[1]

My first encounter with the icon of the crucifixion took place in the narthex of the Hosios Loukas Monastery chapel, near Stiris, Greece. I had read earlier that the mosaic icons there were a thousand years old, but that piece of information had not prepared me for what can only be described as their timelessness. Christ hangs over that door as he has for a millennium, gazing down upon Mary, his mother. John the disciple, on Jesus' left, has a grief-stricken expression which is palpable despite the antiquity of his face.

If one contemplates the composition for more than a moment, it begins to come alive. Jesus says, "Woman, this is your son!" and to the disciple, "This is your mother!"

We tourists did not tarry long there. We were Westerners all, and used to flesh and blood realism. The stylistic device which expresses the divine in human form, narrow nose, wide eyes and exaggerated torso, proved unnerving to some of us. The icon as a "window to heaven" sometimes seems to invite an encounter with the divine before we are quite ready to receive it.

In this light, Anthony M. Coniaris observes, "(the icon) provides an existential encounter between man and God. It becomes the place of an appearance of Christ, provided one stands before it with the right disposition of heart and mind. It becomes a place of prayer. An icon participates in the event it depicts, and is almost a recreation of that event existentially for the believer."[2]

If the crucifixion icon at Hosios Loukas seems timeless, it may be in part because the truth it conveys is one with the newness of the Gospel itself. The subject matter confronts us. It bypasses our intellect and heads straight for our heart. The cross, the skull, the city wall, Jesus' charge to his mother and the beloved disciple — these confront our existential hunger for grace and truth.

The cross is the center of the icon. Jesus does not so much hang on the cross as he is "wedded" to it. He becomes part of the cross and the cross becomes part of him. One's attention is focused on his raised arms and his hands opened in the ancient *orans* attitude of prayer.

Here we are shown the work of suffering love. Kallistos Ware asks us to think on John's account of the Last Supper, which begins with the words, "Before the paschal feast when Jesus knew that the hour had come when he should leave this world and go to the Father, having loved his own who were in the world, he loved them to the end" (13:1). In Greek, *the end* is *eis telos,* meaning, "to the uttermost." The world *telos* is taken up again in Jesus' final cry from the cross, "It is finished." — *tetelestos* (19:30). Although the cry ends in Jesus' death, it is not a cry of despair, but of victory, meaning, "It is accomplished! It is fulfilled"[3] Ware continues, "..his suffering love has a creative effect on me, transforming my own heart and will, releasing me from bondage, making me whole, rendering it possible for me to love in a way that would lie altogether beyond my powers, had I not first been loved by him."[4]

The cross does not release us from suffering. It does not exempt us from suffering. Christ offers us "not a way around suffering but a way through it; not substitution, but saving companionship."[5]

Helen Lemmel's great hymn, *Turn Your Eyes Upon Jesus,* expresses this same truth:

> Thro' death into life everlasting
> He passed, and we follow him there;
> Over us sin no more hath dominion —
> For more than conquerors we are.[6]

Beneath the cross there is a cavern which opens up at the moment of Christ's death to reveal a skull. This detail is in virtually every icon of the crucifixion, and many people are puzzled by it. In early times it was widely believed that the bones of Adam lay buried under Golgotha, the "place of the skull." Iconographers have retained this detail to express the words of Paul in I Corinthians 15:22 — "For as in Adam all die, so also in Christ shall all be made alive."

Here we see the redemption accomplished by the new Adam who makes himself one with the old Adam, to save the human race.[7]

Behind the cross there is a wall. This detail corresponds to historical truth, as John says: "And carrying his own cross he went out of the city..(19:17)." Like all criminals in those days, Jesus suffered outside the walls. Like all criminals, he was taken away from the city to be executed, lest his body render the city, the temple and the executioners unclean.[8]

This detail also expresses a spiritual truth. Just as Christ suffered outside the walls, we must follow him outside the walls of the church. Hebrews 13:12-13 says: "..and so Jesus too suffered outside the gate to sanctify the people with his own blood. Let us go then, outside the camp, and share his degradation."

In the same spirit, George McLeod, founder of Scotland's Iona Community, wrote these words:

> I simply argue that the Cross be raised again at the centre of the market place as well as on the steeple of the church. I am recovering the claim that Jesus was not crucified in a Cathedral between two candles, but on a Cross between two thieves; on the town garbage heap; at a crossroad so cosmopolitan that they had to write his title in Hebrew and in Latin and in Greek (or shall we say in English, in Bantu and in Afrikaans?); at the kind of place where cynics talk smut, and thieves curse, and soldiers gamble. Because that is where he

died. And that is what he died about. And that is where churchmen should be and what church-men should be about.[9]

Now we come to Jesus' charge to his mother and the beloved disciple. Behind this charge is certainly the command, strictly obeyed by the Jews, to "honor thy father and mother."[10]

Here we have the Redeemer of the world, attending to the basic concerns of familial and filial kindness. Even in his last moments he knew that his mother may not have fully comprehended what he was about. Yet she took her stand at the cross even though her doing so may have meant severing ties with the rest of her family.

Here is the Mother of God, the Theotokos, loving her firstborn *eis telos* — to the uttermost; and here is Jesus, concerned that the beloved disciple provide for her what her earthly kin would not provide. As Clovis Chappell has observed, "Home is a place to live; it is a place to love. Lacking this, home is just another name for Hell."[11]

Having nowhere else to go, John took Mary into his home that very hour. He represents the missionary impetus of the Church. Later he would become an apostle to the pagans at Ephesus, and would himself die "outside the walls," after suffering persecution and exile on the island of Patmos.

For Orthodoxy, Mary is the heritage of Israel. Her unbelieving family is superceded by her new family, the Church. In "Behold your mother, " John is saying to the Church, "Do not hold in contempt the heritage which is Israel. Without her, the Church is cut off from its roots and impoverished." In "Behold your son," John is saying to Israel, "your fulfillment is to be found in Christ, within the fellowship of the Church."[12]

For the faithful, the crucifixion icon becomes a window to heaven. It invites us to participate in the event it expresses. But even if we decline, it stands as a witness, as has

100

Orthodoxy herself for well over a millennium. The icon invites us to be engaged by the Mystery. If not now, it will wait for another day.

[1] Ouspensky, Leonid and Lossky, Vladimir, *The Meaning of Icons,* St. Vladimir's Seminary Press, Crestwood, NY., 10707., 1982., p. 180.
[2] Coniaris, Anthony M., Introducing the Orthodox Church, Light and Life Publishing Co., PO Box 26421, Minneapolis, MN 55426-0421., 1982., p. 175.
[3] Ware, Kallistos, *The Orthodox Way,* St. Vladimir's Seminary Press, Crestwood, NY., 1980., p. 107.
[4] Ibid., p. 109.
[5] Ibid., p. 109.
[6] *Youth Worship and Sing.,* Hope Publishing Co., 5705 West Lake Ar., Chicago IL., 1961., p. 113.
[7] Op. Cit., Ouspensky and Lossky., p. 181
[8] Ibid., p. 181.
[9] McLeod, George, *Only One way Left,* Cunningham Lectures, New College, Edinburgh & Auburn Lectures, Union Seminary, NY., 1954., Iona Community (Glasgow), Publisher., p. 38.
[10] Chappell, Clovis G., *The Seven Words.,* Abingdon-Cokesbury Press, NY and Nashville., 1952., p. 31.
[11] Ibid., pps. 32-33.
[12] Marsh, John, *Saint John,* Westminster-Pelican Commentaries, Westminster Press, Philadelphia., 1968., pps. 616-617.

THE HARROWING OF HELL

Today Hades tearfully sighs: 'Would that I had not received Him who was born of Mary, for He came to me and destroyed my power; He broke my bronze gates, and being God, delivered the souls I had been holding captive.' O, Lord, glory to your cross and to your holy resurrection.[1]

Calvin, the little boy in the comic strip *Calvin and Hobbes,* can change himself in his imagination into a fire-breathing dragon, or any other creature. This process he calls "transmogrification," and to a child, the process is very real. In my time, I have witnessed more than a few itinerant evangelists 'transmogrify' themselves into fire-breathing dragons. I retain a vivid childhood memory of one who laid out every paving stone in Hell.

Helmut Thielicke, who has little time for these individuals, sees their histrionics as a way of trying to throw a harness over people. In this, he is in full agreement with Martin Luther, who is said to have remarked, "I think very little of the idea that there is supposed to be a special place where the damned souls are now, as the painters portray it, and the belly-servers preach it."[2]

We may not, however, dismiss the idea of Hell simply because some of those who preach it seem to be flagrant opportunists. There *is* scriptural foundation for it, especially in Matthew's Gospel where Jesus talks about hellfire (5:22); the outer darkness where there will be weeping and grinding of teeth (22:13); and the frightful time when everyone must render an account for what he or she has done (12:36; 25:19).

It is foolish however, to try to localize Hell. In Marlowe's *Doctor Faustus,* Faust asks his infernal companion Mephistopheles how he can be working his mischief on earth since he is said to have been chained eternally in Hell. Mephistopheles replies, "Why this is hell, nor am I out of it."[3]

105

Thielicke, who lived through Hell in all of its forms in Nazi Germany, has done much to "rehabilitate" it. He writes:

> ..it is impossible to localize hell (and) it is also impossible to name the dates at which it begins for us. Hell is certainly not to be relegated solely to the time *after* death or *after* the last Judgment. It can draw us into its demonic field of force right now..(It) is separation from God in all of its forms. It is ultimate forsakenness.[4]

To speak of Hell at all, we must speak in analogies. When we speak of Hell as a place of torture or pain, we are attempting to explain a state of being we cannot fully know this side of the grave, by way of images and states with which we are already familiar.[5] Everyone knows that any analogy eventually breaks down. How much more must earthly analogies of things that are not fully of this world lead to confusion and distortions?[6]

Thomas Merton speaks of Hell using the familiar analogy of fire:

> Our God also is a consuming fire, and if we, by love, become transformed into Him and burn as He burns, His fire will be our everlasting joy. But if we refuse His love and remain in the coldness of sin and opposition to Him and to other men, then will His fire (by our own choice rather than His) become our everlasting enemy, and love instead of being our joy will become our torment and our destruction.[7]

When we are against God, when we love ourselves more than him, all things become our enemies.[8]

What does separation from God look like? I have a colleague in the ministry who nearly died on the operating table during open-heart surgery. He tells of waking up in a wooded glen where trees were leafy and green but the color of a vulgar neon. The sky was blue, but of a glacial hue. The sun was shining, but with the glare not unlike the glare of an operating table-lamp. There were tables set with food, but it too was strange, like those plaster facsimiles of food one sees in store refrigerator displays. There was a crowd of people waiting to be fed, but from the shrillness of their voices it was evident that they hated one another. But when anyone tried to leave, they tugged and pulled to prevent that from happening. Suddenly they began tugging at my colleague, and he knew that unless he escaped their clutches, they would destroy him forever. Suddenly he realized that the light was not the sun, but the harsh light of the recovery room. He grasped his wife's hand and whispered, "I think I've just been in Hell!"

Merton gives us much the same picture when he says:

> Hell is where no one has anything in common
> with anybody else except for the fact that they all
> hate one another and cannot get away from one
> another and themselves.[9]

Put another way, Hell is self-love carried to its ultimate conclusion, which is the end of all joy and meaning. Hell may be found in other people certainly, but more significantly, hell is myself, cut off from others by reason of my own self-centeredness.[10]

Hell is being sadder but wiser about a wrong decision that cannot be changed, about the stakes we have lost during a game that is now over.[11]

There is a finality about Hell. Thielicke continues:

> ..the terrifying thing about hell is not the blisters
> one gets from the alleged fire there. The real terror
> comes from being devoured by the pangs of a
> conscience that knows no forgiveness.[12]

107

But just suppose God has other ways of reaching us — ways we cannot now imagine because they are beyond the range of experiences of this earthly life. This is the meaning behind this pericope from the writings of the apostle Peter: "He went and preached to the spirits in prison" (I Peter 3:19). This text provides the basis for the seventh article of the Apostles' Creed, which some Protestant denominations have chosen to omit. The article in question is "He descended into Hell."[13]

I do not suggest that a "Purgatory" might actually exist. Orthodoxy itself has rejected such a notion, and few Protestants would entertain it for a moment. I argue only that Divine love is everywhere, and that this is what the Psalmist had in mind when he wrote, "If I ascend into heaven, you are there, there too, if I lie in hell" (Psalm 139:8).

This idea is represented in the *Harrowing of Hell* icon. When I first encountered it, it greatly offended my Protestant sensibilities, but it too is an analogy which expresses a mystery that might otherwise be inaccessible to us.

In the icon, Christ appears in Hell, not as its captive, but as its conqueror, and the deliverer of those imprisoned therein. He tramples the crossed panels of Hell's doors underfoot, and stands astride the abyss. In his left hand he holds a scroll — symbol of the Word. With his right hand he snatches Adam from his grave. Eve follows, as do all who waited for his coming in faith.

Thielicke suggests that Christ is saying *this* to all who meditate on this pericope:

> For me..the Lord over both the living and the dead, no limit exists, so that my mercy may prevail. And I know how to find even the dead who call to me..and who now have been forsaken by their fetishes and their idols; all those who were carried off in childhood and died prematurely; the atheists who were withdrawn from my word and heard only a distorted caricature of it. I

cannot let these lost souls go. My suffering was great enough to make up for them too.[14]

Kallistos Ware asks, "How can a love of God accept that even a single one of his creatures whom he has made should remain forever in hell?"[15] Divine love is everywhere. It rejects no one, even though we are free to reject divine love. We cannot however, do this without inflicting pain on ourselves, and the more determined our rejection, the greater our suffering.[16]

We began with an image of the "evangelist" who "transmogrifies" into a fire-breathing dragon. This is my childhood image of God, which I suspect lurks somewhere within the "child" of all of us. I suggest that we begin to let this childhood image go, that another may begin to grow in its place. Perhaps an illustration may help:

I was not in college very long before I noticed the "bag lady." Everyone knew her, for she was the only bag lady in that small college town. She was everywhere: at the shopping center dumpster early in the morning, and in the campus quadrangle by early afternoon, arguing with the pigeons. Almost every evening she could be seen in the campus cafeteria having dinner with a tweedy and distinguished-looking professor who turned out to be her husband of many years.

Gradually the pieces of the puzzle came together. Some of the older faculty members recalled that when she was a lovely young woman, she sang, "He Shall Feed His Flock," at the Presbyterian Church. She couldn't have been much company for the professor. Every evening he pointed his bullet-nosed Studebaker toward town and drove up and down every street until he found her. You might say that she lived in hell. It was a Hell that she had more or less created for herself, but Hell nonetheless. She had abandoned the professor for drink many years earlier, but he never abandoned her.

If you looked carefully you could see in his face the very image of Christ — and this Christ will find us, even in Hell. We may forsake Christ, but he will never forsake us.

1   *Byzantine Daily Worship,* Alleluia Press, PO Box 103., Allendale NJ., 07401., p. 835. Blessing of the New Light., Idiomela (Eighth tone), no. 2.

2   Thielicke, Helmut, *I Believe: The Christian's Creed,* Fortress Press, Philadelphia., 1968., p. 124.

3   Ibid., p. 127.

4   Ibid., p. 124.

5   Patrinacos, Nicon D., *A Dictionary of Greek Orthodoxy,* Hellenic Heritage Publications, Pleasantville, NY., 10507., 1984., p. 188.

6   Op. Cit., Thielicke., p. 123.

7   Merton, Thomas, *New Seeds of Contemplation,* New Directions, 80 Eighth Ave., NY., 10011., p. 124.

8   Ibid., p. 124.

9   Ibid., p. 123.

10 Op. Cit., Thielicke., p. 124.

11 Ibid., p. 128.

12 Ibid., p. 124.

13 Outler, Albert, Ed., *John Wesley,* Oxford University Press, NY., 1964., p. 495 i.e., "Wesley is everywhere unemphatic about the addition to the Apostles' Creed of the phrase, 'he descended into Hell,' possibly because of its consistent absence from the early texts. In at least one version of his 'Sunday Service' it was simply dropped out; it was then omitted in subsequent usage in the American Methodist Church. Cf. Wesley's pallid comment on I Peter 3:18-19 in his *Explanatory Notes Upon the New Testament (1775);* see also J.N.D. Kelly, *Early Christian Creeds* (1950), 378-383."

14 Op. Cit., Thielicke., p. 132.

15 Ware, Kallistos, *The Orthodox Way,* St. Vladimir's Seminary Press., Crestwood, NY., 10707., 1980., p. 181.

16 Ibid., p. 182.

THE MYRRH-BEARING WOMEN

Mary and her companions went forth before
dawn: they found the stone rolled away from the
tomb and heard the angel say: 'Why do you seek
Him as a man among the dead when He is in eternal splendor? Behold, the shroud is folded.
Hasten, and proclaim to the world that the Lord is
risen and has crushed death, for He is the Son of
God, the Saviour of Mankind.'[1]

The icon of the myrrh-bearing women conveys an
"austere, calm solemnity,"[2] in that the resurrection itself is
beyond comprehension and inaccessible to the eye. When
we speak of the resurrection, we must refer either to the
"before" or the "after," because the event itself lies within
an aura of silence and is shrouded in a veil of mystery."[3] According to Matthew's telling, (28:1-8) the angel has removed
the stone, not to permit the risen Christ to come out of the
tomb, as had been necessary at the raising of Lazarus, but
"..to show he was no longer in the sepulchre and to enable
the women to see that the resurrection had already taken
place."[4]

Every detail in this icon contributes to this austere
solemnity. The angel and the angel's message, the dismay of
the women, and the state of the grave clothes tell us that
"..the day of resurrection is the beginning of days outside
time, that is, an indication of the mystery of the future life,
the Kingdom of the Holy Spirit, where God is 'all in all.' "[5]

The scene is dominated by the angel of the resurrection.
This is the same figure Mark identifies as "the young man in
white" (16:5). In Matthew's telling, however, the figure is of
supernatural aspect, like Jesus at his Transfiguration, or the
angel of Revelation (10:1) — "wrapped in a cloud, with a
rainbow over his head; his face..like the sun, and his
legs..pillars of fire."

The angel is a messenger of power. His descent shakes the earth. His hands easily roll away the massive stone. He takes his seat upon it as if it were a throne befitting one whose authority comes from the Father. In his face is lightning that shatters the gloom of night, revealing the shapes of hidden things. His robe is white as snow — a supernatural contrast to the darkness of human frailty. The guards who "become as dead men" are not depicted. Someone recently asked me about this. "If the icon is supposed to be a faithful rendering of the Matthean account, why are the guards not in the picture?" Only those details essential to the salvation story are included. Persons who are dead in their sins are not part of the "picture" of salvation until they begin to awaken to the Light of the World.

The angel's message, "There is no need for you to be afraid, I know you are looking for Jesus who was crucified. He is not here, for he has risen, as he said he would," links the resurrection to Jesus' three predictions of his suffering found in this gospel (16:21; 17:23; and 20:23). In the first, Peter had said, "Heaven forbid, Lord..this must not happen to you." In the second, great sadness comes over the disciples, and in the third, they quarrel over the best seats in the kingdom. In a word, they comprehended none of it. The angel points to the empty sepulchre with a gesture less comforting than commanding, which says, "Now you *will* understand!"

Why is this majestic figure giving audience to these women and not to the disciples? In the world of the New Testament, women are weak and insignificant. They are of no account, like Luke's shepherds who hear the angels sing. The disciples had been concerned about "best seats" and privileges. These women had been content to love Jesus. This is why they receive the angel's message. The disciples are not yet ready to receive it!

We learn from Luke (8:1-3) that one of the women, Mary Magdalene, had been possessed by seven demons. Having grappled with a demon or two in my own life, I know that one demon is debilitating enough. But seven? Yet Mary's weakness does not exclude her from receiving the angel's message. In fact, it prepares her to receive it. Nor shall any depth of sin separate us from the love of Christ!

The other woman, identified only as "the other Mary," may be the mother of James, son of Alphaeus (Matthew 10:3), but there is no certainty as to her identity. I once lived in a college community where another student had the same name as mine. More than once I was referred to as "the other one," and whenever this occurred, I felt rather insignificant. I felt worse than that when I began to get his bills. (His grades weren't so hot either!)

The other Mary has no status of her own. Her identity is linked to that of another, apart from whom she would have no identity at all. So it is with the disciple of Jesus — our status is borrowed. If we have trouble accepting this relationship, we may be very far from the kingdom of God.

We see that the two Marys are well aware of their weakness and insignificance, and would, if they could, hide behind the frame of the icon. They will, however, remain in the resurrection drama by virtue of their love for Christ. They are at the tomb because of their love's protest against death. They will certainly remain after they have seen the love that is the death of Death!

You will notice that the graveclothes retain the form they had when the body of the Lord remained in them. This detail is a protest against the rumor circulated by the priests and the elders that the disciples had secreted the body away (Matthew 28:13). It is this detail that causes the beloved disciple in John's gospel to see and believe (20:8).

In no respect is this a "media event." It is an event that is perceived in time, yet takes place beyond time. It cannot be perceived as "occurring," and yet it has occurred, and will yet occur. Not only has time not abolished belief in this event. In truth, this event abolishes time. It is an event of such enormity that it cannot be easily denied, yet its acceptance demands a tremendous suspension of disbelief.

117

For Paul, the resurrection is the key to our future in God, as he indicates in I Corinthians 15:19, "If our hope in Christ has been for this life only, we are indeed the most miserable of people."

Helmut Thielicke, in a resurrection sermon, puts it this way:

> If Jesus lives and rules, then I am, for example, no longer completely without hope. My cares are driven away. Then I know that my loved ones have not passed away from me but have passed on to him. I do not have to take much of the disappointment in my life so terribly seriously any more.[6]

The day we begin to believe in the resurrection is the day the universe changes. It is the day we begin to believe that Christ can heal our wounds, forgive our sins, and roll away the stone from our tomb. It is the day we step out of time and time's bondage to decay. It is the day we begin to participate in the mystery of the future life — the kingdom of the Holy Spirit, where God is all in all.

[1] *Byzantine Daily Worship,* Alleluia Press., PO Box 103., Allendale, NJ., 07401. 1969., p. 849. Hypacoi (Fourth Tone).

[2] Ouspensky, Leonid and Lossky, Vladimir, *The Meaning of Icons,* St. Vladimir's Seminary Press, Crestwood, NY., 1982., p. 189.

[3] Ibid., p. 189.

[4] Ibid., p. 189.

[5] Ibid., p. 192.

[6] Thielicke, Helmut, *I Believe — The Christian's Creed,* Fortress Press., Philadelphia., 1968., pps. 149-150.

THE ASCENSION

Christ our God who gloriously ascended into
heaven and gladdened your disciples with the
power of the Holy Spirit: Through your blessing,
You confirmed them in their belief that You are
truly the Son of God, the Redeemer of the World.[1]

The icon of the Ascension commemorates the ascending
of Christ into heaven as witnessed by the apostles. This took
place on the Mount of Olives on the fortieth day after the
resurrection. For the Orthodox, the ascension marks the
completion of the great cycle of salvation and witnesses to
that contagious and renewing movement in the Spirit which
is at work reconciling the whole created order to God.
Leonid Ouspensky writes of this event, "The centre of gravi-
ty in the accounts of the Holy Scripture and consequently of
the iconography (of the feast) lies not in the fact of the
Ascension itself, but in the significance and consequences it
has for the Church and the world."[2] By "significance and
consequences" he refers to the central tenet of Orthodoxy,
as first expressed by Irenaeus and Athanasius. "God became
man in order that man might become God."[4]

From a Protestant point of view, the idea of the deification of matter, to which this certainly refers, seems strange if
not unbiblical. It is, as I hope to demonstrate, quite biblical
and consistent with the Wesleyan doctrine of the Christian
perfection as expressed in the hymnody of Charles Wesley:

Finish then thy new creation;
Pure and spotless let us be.
Let us see the great salvation
perfectly restored in thee.[4]

Hendrikus Berkhof, in his little book *Well Founded
Hope*, says much the same thing:

First Jesus was present among us in the manner of a bodily human presence as the only representative of a new humanity. Now he is present among us in the Spirit, through whom he works in a contagious and renewing movement to conform many people to his image. And soon the harvest of this process will be gathered, when he will appear as the center of a world which is re-created in his own image.[5]

The icon of the Ascension bespeaks a continuity between this world and the next — a new heaven and a new earth. We are not saved *from* this body, but *in* it. We are not saved *from* the material world, but *in* it.[6] Our own salvation involves the transfiguration of the whole animate and inanimate order. This means that there is a place in the age to come for *all* creation, humans, animals, plants and trees, rocks, fire and water.[7] Paul alludes to this eventuality when he says:

> For we know that the whole of creation has been groaning and suffering as if in childbirth until now; and not only the creation but we ourselves, who have the firstfruits of the Spirit, groan inwardly as we wait for adoption as sons, for the redemption of our bodies" (Romans 8:22-23).

Much of Protestantism, I fear, has emphasized the discontinuity between this world and the next at the expense of the continuity. It is perfectly true that Paul states, and emphatically too, that "flesh and blood cannot inherit the kingdom of God" (I Corinthians 15:50). In the very next verse, however, he alludes to that part of the mystery of the divine economy that allows for continuity as well as discontinuity. He says, just as emphatically, "..we are not at all going to die, but we shall all be changed"(I Cor. 15:51).

The resurrection means a radical renovation (discontinuity), but not something totally new (continuity). Prof. Berkhof states in affirmation of this faith, "I will rise again, as a completely new person," and, "I will rise again, as the same being."[8]

When I first answered the call to the Christian ministry, I felt profoundly unworthy, even morbidly so. When folks began to call me "Reverend" I found myself in the midst of a kind of spiritual paralysis. I had the normal urges of any young man, which were leaving me with a tremendous measure of guilt. Then there were the rigors of theological education. I had never been a "good " student and this inadequacy only heightened my sense of unworthiness. One day it happened that a chapel speaker had chosen I Corinthians 15:51 for his text. It was almost as though he had intended his message for me, for he said, "When God called you, it was *you* he called." My insecurities, uncertainties and perceived inadequacies did not immediately dissolve as the morning fog, but some light did penetrate my troubled spirit. I was being told that God wanted me just as I was. Discontinuity began to give way to continuity, and I began to discover that both are part of the mystery.

In the icon of the Ascension, this paradox is expressed in a most revealing way. The risen Savior abides beyond the limits of history, yet remains present within the historical process. The upper and lower parts of the icon form, as it were, a continuum. Both parts — the earthly and the heavenly — penetrate one another. The risen Savior, through the contagious and renewing movement of the Spirit, is the bearer of light and life. Charles Wesley, for his part, expresses this mystery in this familiar hymn text:

Light and life to all he brings,
Risen with healing in his wings...[9]

We, who inhabit the earthly portion of the continuum, are flesh, albeit created in the image of God. We, as individual members of Christ's body the Church, are granted the gift of grace which enables us to be raised from spiritual paralysis to participation in the image of God. God the Creator yearns for union with creation because God is love. Similarly, creation yearns for union with the Creator despite the defacement of the divine image in creation due to sin. In Christ, the divine image is restored.

I would like now to examine the figures represented in the composition of this icon. This composition, incidentally, has remained virtually the same for more than fifteen hundred years, which gives some indication of its depth of meaning.

Christ ascends, enveloped in a mandorla, which is an iconographic device used to depict the clouds of heaven. This same device we have already encountered in the icon of the Transfiguration. It is composed of several concentric circles which represent the pre-Copernican view of the visible sky. When one first encounters this icon it seems that Christ is in the process of discarding his earthly existence like the first stage of a booster rocket. The upward movement, however, does not indicate that the risen Christ is in the process of leaving. The icon is not to be seen as one frame of motion picture film frozen in stop-action, which would have Christ disappear into the stratosphere the moment the reels begin turning again. The icon does not depict the heavenly and earthly realms drawing apart. Quite the contrary! In the icon, the heavenly and earthly realms are undergoing a deep, inner connection.

Christ's blessing is not to be construed as a gesture of farewell, but an expression of this connection. Of course, Acts 1:9 does state, "..he was lifted up while they looked on, and a cloud took him from their sight." This, however, must be seen in the light of Matthew 28:20, "And know that I am with you always; yes, to the end of time." In Christ, the heavenly and earthly realms penetrate one another, and yet they are separated, and will remain so until the inauguration of that great event of crisis and renewal which will come with Christ's return. He holds a scroll in his left hand. This indicates that he remains not only the source of blessing but the source of knowledge. Ignorance of the Word is darkness. Knowledge of the Word is light, and the darkness does not overpower it (John 1:9).

The two angels, one on the right, and the other on the left of the mandorla, seem to be raising Christ of their own strength, but they are there for quite another purpose — to testify that the invisible as well as the visible realm gives praise. We Protestants have difficulty seeing angels as anything more than a decorative touch. But they are far more than that. They represent all that remains unseen, unperceived and unheard. They represent all that is mysterious, all that is hidden and all that we cannot know. The icon says that even these realms give praise.

The Mother of God is positioned immediately below the ascending Christ in virtually all of the icons of the Ascension. She, for the Orthodox, is the personification of the Church. She is the one who had been counted worthy to take God into herself and, through her obedience, become the Temple of the Incarnate Word.[10] Her hands are uplifted in the ancient *orans* position of prayer, a gesture which expresses the intercession of the Church on behalf of all creation.

She is flanked by the two angels mentioned in Acts 1:11, who point upward and ask the apostles, "Why are you men from Galilee standing there looking into the sky? Jesus who has been taken up from you into heaven, this same Jesus will come back in the same way as you have seen him go there." Their number is two because the Jewish legal system required the testimony of two to establish a case (II Corinthians 13:1).

The apostles are positioned into two groups of six. In some icons they gesticulate wildly, which provides tension in an icon otherwise so devoid of tension. Their diversity of gestures represents the diversity of human personality, the diversity of spiritual gifts, and the diversity of tongues, soon to be poured out at Pentecost. This diversity must not only be tolerated in the church, but actively encouraged, lest dour uniformity be equated with zeal for the Gospel.

Paul, who could not possibly have been present at the actual Ascension, is depicted. Although "untimely born," he, more than any of the apostles, represents the Gentile mission of the Church. He is situated on the right, close to the Mother of God.

Peter, to the left of the Mother of God, symbolizes the Jerusalem Church, tied to its Jewish heritage, but no less part of the whole. These two apostles are a further expression of the continuity/discontinuity theme. Peter represents continuity with the children of Abraham. Paul represents discontinuity, the spiritual truth that God can raise new children for Abraham from stones.

As I indicated earlier, the ascension of the deified human body of the Savior reveals the possibility of the deification of humankind through the descent of the Spirit. Vladimir Lossky indicates that this ascent is composed of two stages, achieved simultaneously on two different but closely interrelated levels — action (praxis) and contemplation (theoria). The two, he states, "are inseparable in Christian knowledge, which is a personal and conscious experience of spiritual realities."[11]

Many Protestants find the notion of "deification" akin to works-righteousness. Works-righteousness, however, cannot express the spirit of joy made visible by the gift of grace.

The idea of the deification of matter was not alien to Charles Wesley, who says in the hymn text *Spirit of Faith Come Down:*

Inspire the living faith
which who so-e'er receives
The witness in himself he hath
And consciously believes;

That faith that conquers all,
And doth the mountain move,
And saves who-e'er on Jesus call,
And perfects them in love.[12]

Another, more familiar Wesleyan hymn text shows the same affinity to Orthodox belief:

Come let us rise with Christ our Head
And seek the things above,
By the almighty spirit led
And filled with faith and love;
Our hearts detached from all below
Should after him ascend,
And only wish the joy to know
Of our triumphant friend.[13]

The question that we must ask is, "When does this future crisis of renewal happen? Does it occur beyond the borders of our own death? How does this relate to the Second Coming? What of those who have not believed?"

Again, Professor Berkhof provides some clarity:

The future...and certainly the transition to that future, is an event, a process. But we, standing on this side of that process, are not able to map it out chronologically. We will therefore speak of..four themes, resurrection, second coming, judgment and life everlasting, mainly as approximations of the one indivisible reality.[14]

Everyone who hopes in Christ looks toward this indivisible reality, not with dread, but with eager anticipation. It (and we cannot know precisely what *it* is) may be as natural for the person of faith as leaving one room and entering another. But without this hope, only judgment and lostness will be disclosed. "All lives," Professor Berkhof continues, "that were lived against the grain of God's intention for the world will be inexorably disclosed...in their lostness."[15]

The icon of the Ascension, for all it implies, maintains a mood of sober reserve. It is with the same reserve that I John 3:2 expresses the hope it reveals:

> Beloved ones, we are now the children of God but it has not been revealed to us what we shall be in the future; but we do know that when he appears we shall be like him, for we shall see him as he really is.

For now, all we can say is what Paul said in his first Corinthian letter:

> The nature of that earth-born man is shared by his earthly sons, the nature of the heaven-born man by his heavenly sons; and it remains for us, who once bore the stamp of earth, to bear the stamp of heaven (15:48-49).

[1] *Byzantine Daily Worship,* Alleluia Press, PO Box 103., Allendale NJ., 07401. 1969., p. 885. Troparion of the Feast of the Ascension-Fourth Tone.
[2] Ouspensky, Leonid and Lossky, Vladimir, *The Meaning of Icons,* St. Vladimir's Seminary Press, Crestwood, NY., 10707., 1982., p. 194.
[3] Lossky, Vladimir, *The Mystical Theology of the Eastern Church,* St. Vladimir's Seminary Press, Crestwood, NY., 10707., 1976., p. 134.
[4] *The Methodist Hymnal,* The Methodist Publishing House, Nashville., TN., 1964., #283.
[5] Berkhof, Hendrikus, *Well-Founded Hope,* John Knox Press, Richmond, VA., 1969., p. 41.
[6] Ware, Kallistos, *The Orthodox Way.,* St. Vladimir's Seminary Press., Crestwood, NY., 10707., p. 183.
[7] Ibid., p. 183.
[8] Op. Cit., Berkhof., p. 37.
[9] Op. Cit., *The Methodist Hymnal,* #388.
[10] Op. Cit., Lossky and Ouspensky., p. 196.
[11] Op. Cit., Lossky, p. 202.
[12] Op. Cit., *The Methodist Hymnal.,* #137.
[13] Ibid., #457.
[14] Op. Cit., Berkhof., p. 32.
[15] Ibid., p. 46.

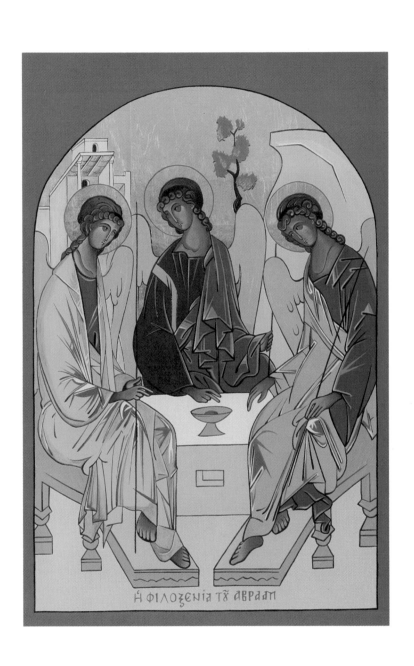

Ἡ ΦΙΛΟΞΕΝΙΑ ΤΫ ΑΒΡΑΑΜ

THE OLD TESTAMENT TRINITY

> We have seen the true light, we have received the
> heavenly Spirit, we have found the true faith!
> Wherefore we worship the undivided Trinity for
> having saved us.[1]

For the Orthodox, Pentecost is not only a celebration of
the outpouring of the Holy Spirit (Acts 2:1-13) but primarily
a celebration of the Holy Trinity. The day most Protestants
call Pentecost Sunday the Orthodox call Trinity Day. On
this day, the icon of the Holy Trinity is brought out for worship. Commemoration of the Descent of the Holy Spirit on
the Apostles occurs the next day. Then it is that the icon of
the Descent of the Holy Spirit is brought out. We will
discuss this commemoration, and its accompanying icon, in
the next chapter.

Leonid Ouspensky emphasizes the importance of Trinity
Day for the Orthodox:

> If, on the day of the Lord's baptism, the manifesta-
> tion of the Holy Trinity was accessible only to the
> external senses, John the Baptist heard the voice
> of the Father, and saw the Son and the Holy Spirit
> descending in the physical form of a dove; today,
> the grace of the Holy Spirit, giving light to the
> whole being of man redeemed by the Son of God,
> brings him to deification.[2]

Of deification we will say more later. Suffice it to say
here that nowhere is the possibility of humankind's ascent
to the Divine brought into sharper focus and, the Orthodox
believe, to greater possibility than in contemplation of the
Trinity.

The Trinity — Father, Son, and Holy Spirit — has neither
beginning nor ending in time. The Son was begotten of the

Father, says the Nicene Creed, before all worlds. So too the Spirit proceeds from the Father. It is this timelessness that the icon of the Trinity seeks to convey.

Our first encounter with the Triune God of scripture is found in the first creation narrative of Genesis 1:26 where the Father says, "Let us make man in our own image, in the likeness of ourselves". Our second comes in the eighteenth chapter at the point where three heavenly visitors appear to Abraham and Sarah at the Oak of Mamre, with news concerning the birth of their son Isaac. For the Orthodox, this first manifestation of the Trinity is the beginning of a promise that will find its fulfillment on the Day of Pentecost. It is evidence that the Old Covenant prefigures the New, and that the new finds it completion in the doctrine of the Trinity.

In the icon, the heavenly visitors appear as winged beings. This is an iconographic device which identifies the visitors as messengers from the heavenly realm. John the Baptist, himself a heavenly messenger, is sometimes depicted as a winged being.

We notice that in the icon, the figures of Abraham and Sarah do not appear. Iconographers have tended to underplay the presence of the other participants in the Genesis story since the appearance, in the early Fifteenth Century, of Andrei Rublev's world-renowned icon, "The Old Testament Trinity" (Tretyakov Gallery, Moscow).[3] The composition here depicted is after the manner of Rublev. The heavenly visitors form an unseen circle, in the center of which is the chalice of sacrifice. The circle expresses the unity within the Godhead and suggests the heavenly mandorla. The mandorla, as I indicated earlier, is a device used to express the divine source of the revelation as in the Transfiguration and the Harrowing of Hell. It also appears in the Dormition of the Virgin, which we shall consider later.

Western Christendom is accustomed to seeing the Trinity depicted as three intertwined circles, or a triangle in the center of three intertwined circles. So graphic a depiction of the Trinity as this undoubtedly seems strange if not suspect. We must be aware that the three heavenly messengers are not a representation of the Trinity itself since in its essence the Godhead cannot be represented. The icon is intended to reveal the unity and triunity of the Godhead by having the worshipper contemplate its triune action in the world.[4]

An expression such as "the essence of the Godhead" may be troublesome to us, so perhaps a brief presentation of the theology of the Trinity might be helpful. It is important here to know that the Greek Fathers always maintained that the Trinity must be Revelation before it can be speculation. By that I mean, the mystery of God must be encountered before "theologizing" is appropriate, or even possible. The nomenclature which developed over many centuries to express the mystery of the Trinity must from the outset be seen as limited and inadequate.

John Meyendorff underscores the truth that any discussion of the Trinity must be preceded by encounter. "The Fathers always maintained that we cannot know *what* God is, only *that* God is, (italics mine) because he has revealed himself, in salvation history, as Father, Son, and Holy Spirit."[5] Further, "The incarnate Logos (Word) and the Holy Spirit are met and experienced first as the divine agents of salvation, and only then are they discovered to be essentially one God."[6]

The Greek Fathers believed that this is the best and only possible description of the divine mystery: God is one essence (ousia) and three persons (hypostases).[7] The words *ousia* and *hypostasis* were drawn from Greek philosophy. But here they are used "to distinguish in God that which is common, *ousia,* substance or essence, from that which is particular, *hypostasis,* person."[8] *Ousia* is defined as "all that subsists by itself and which has not its being in another."[9] *Hypostasis,* person, is defined as an agent, "possessing" its own nature and "acting" accordingly.[10] The Father is conceived as a creative agent while the Son and Holy Spirit are conceived in terms of their relationship with the Father. The

Son is "begotten" by the Father, while the Spirit "proceeds" from the Father.

The Greek Fathers speculate about the nature of the Trinity while at the same time they understand that words cannot adequately express so great a mystery. Occasionally they reveal a wonder that borders on frustration. John of Damascus says, for instance, "..the Godhead is undivided; and it it just like three suns cleaving to each other without separation, and giving out light mingled and conjoined into one."[11] Further, "..we have been told that there is a difference between generation (begottenness) and procession, but what is the nature of this difference we do not understand at all."[12] Frustration is clearly apparent in Gregory of Nazianzen, who says, "You ask, 'what is procession from the Holy Spirit?' Do you tell me first what is the unbegottenness of the Father, and I will then explain to you the physiology of the generation of the Son, and the procession of the Spirit, and we shall both of us be stricken with madness for prying into the mystery of God."[13]

The doctrine of the Trinity does tell us that in God there is something analogous to "society."[14] It affirms that just as human life becomes authentic and personal as it is shared, so God "is not a single person dwelling alone, but three persons who share each others' life in perfect love."[15] Just as the three persons of the Trinity live in community, in and for each other, so we become more authentic when we make others' joys and sorrows our own and see, as much as we are able, the world through others' eyes.[16] Each human being is unique, yet each is intended by the Father for communication with others. We first hear of this Divine intention in the second creation account (Genesis 2:18) where God says, "It is not good that the man (human being) should be alone." Irenaeus indicates that the Triune God is *in* community and for community when he says that the Son and the Spirit are "the two hands of the Father." Kallistos Ware indicates that in every creative and sanctifying act, the Father is using both these 'hands' at once.[17]

138

From this it is but one short step to the Wesleyan doctrine of Holiness or Christian Perfection. Albert Outler, the renowned Wesley scholar, tells us that if Wesley's writings about active holiness in this life are to be taken seriously, they become intelligible only in light of their indirect sources in the spirituality of the Greek Fathers.[18] It is no coincidence that St. Macarius of Egypt and Wesley are of one mind where it concerns holiness in light of the Trinitarian image. The saint says, "There is no other way to be saved except through our neighbor...this is purity of heart: when you see the sinful or the sick, to feel compassion for them and be tenderhearted toward them."[19] This resembles the "social holiness" so dear to the heart of Wesley and the early Methodists. This social holiness is the heart of the life of the Trinity. Without it, there is no Christianity at all. Wesley says, "The gospel of Christ knows no religion but social: no holiness but social holiness."[20]

For Wesley, as well as the Greek Fathers, holiness meant nothing less than the restoration of the original image of God in humankind. This reality is expressed in a continual love which becomes one's higher nature and embraces both the Divine and the human, both the Creator and the Created. It knows "no greater task in life than to offer every thought, word and deed as a continual sacrifice to God through Jesus Christ."[21] Thus we find in Wesley's Christian Perfection something analogous to the "ascent," or "deification."

This begins as an encounter with the Triune God. Wesley describes this assurance in words that could very well have been drawn from the Damascene vision of the Trinity as "three suns cleaving together." He says, "..The Spirit of God does give a believer such a testimony of his adoption, that while it is present to the soul, he can no more doubt the reality of his sonship than he can doubt the shining of the sun, while he stands in the full blaze of its beams."[22]

This Trinitarian vision found itself into the hymnody of Wesley's brother Charles:

Father, in whom we live
in whom we are, and move,
The glory, power, and praise receive
For thy creating love.

Incarnate Deity,
Let all the ransomed race
Render in thanks their lives to thee
For thy redeeming grace.

Spirit of holiness,
Let all thy saints adore
Thy sacred energy, and bless
Thine heart-renewing power.

Eternal, Triune Lord,
Let all the hosts above
Let all the sons of men record
And dwell upon thy love.[23]

The mystery of the Trinity must be Revelation before it can be speculation. The Trinity is an expression of the Holiness of God, and the Holy, as I indicated earlier, eludes definition. The richness of the Trinity cannot be demonstrated by human reason but by faith's action in the world.

For the Orthodox, the Trinity is the source of all religious experience, all theology, and all social action. Vladimir Lossky says. "It is Trinity that we seek in seeking after God, when we search for the fullness of being, for the end and meaning of all existence."[24]

Evagrius Ponticus provides, for this discussion, the last word, "To know the mystery of the Trinity in its fullness is to enter into perfect union with God and to attain unto the deification of the human creature: in other words, to enter into the divine life, the very life of the Trinity, and to become, in St. Peter's words, 'partakers of the divine nature.' "[25]

[1] *Byzantine Daily Worship,* Alleluia Press, PO Box 103, Allendale, NJ., 07401. 1969., p. 891. Stitchera of Pentecost (Second tone).

[2] Ouspensky, Leonid and Lossky, Vladimir, *The Meaning of Icons,* St. Vladimir's Seminary Press, Crestwood, NY., 10707., 1982., p. 200.

[3] Sendler, S.J., Egon, *The Icon: Image of the Invisible,* Oakwood Publications, 616 Knob Hill Avenue, Redondo Beach, CA., 90277., pp. 104-105.

[4] Op Cit., Ouspensky and Lossky., p. 202.

[5] Meyendorff, John, *Byzantine Theology: Historical Trends & Doctrinal Themes,* Fordham University Press., NY., 1974., p. 182.

[6] Ibid., p. 180.

[7] Ibid., p. 132.

[8] Lossky, Vladimir, *The Mystical Theology of the Eastern Church,* St. Vladimir's Seminary Press, Crestwood, NY., 10707., 1976., p. 51.

[9] Ibid., p. 50.

[10] Op. Cit., Meyendorff., p. 182.

[11] Op. Cit., Lossky, p. 54, from De Fide Orthodoxa, I, 8', P.G., XCIV., p. 829.

[12] Ware, Kallistos, *The Orthodox Way,* St. Vladimir's Seminary Press, Crestwood, NY., 10707., 1980., p. 43.

[13] Op. Cit., Lossky., p. 55, Oratio XXXI (Theologica V), 8', P.G., XXXVI, 141 B.

[14] Op. Cit., Ware., p. 33.

[15] Ibid., Ware., p. 97.

[16] Ibid., Ware., p. 68.

[17] Ibid., p. 44.

[18] Outler, Ablert, Ed., *John Wesley,* Oxford University Press, Ny., 1964., p. 252.

[19] Op. Cit., Ware., p. 68., from *The Homilies of St. Macarius.*

[20] De Wolf, L. Harold, *A Theology of the Living Church,* Harper and Row, NY and Evanston, 1968., p. 320., as quoted in Flew, R. Newton, et al, *The Nature of the Christian Church According to the Teachings of the Methodists,* London; the Methodist Publishing House, 1936., p. 13., from *Poetical Works of John and Charles Wesley,* I, 22.

[21] Schmidt, Martin, *John Wesley: A Theological Biography,* Vol. II, Part 2., Abingdon Press, Nashville and NY., p. 28.

[22] Sugden, Edward H., Ed., *Wesley's Standard Sermons,* Vol. I, London: The Epworth Press., 1966., X:I:12., p. 210.

[23] *The Methodist Hymnal,* The Methodist Publishing House, Nashville, TN., 1964., #465.

[24] Op. Cit., Lossky., p. 65.

[25] Ibid., Lossky., p. 67.

THE DESCENT OF THE SPIRIT

In days of old, pride brought confusion of tongues to the builders of the tower of Babel, but now the diversity of tongues enlightened the minds and gave knowledge for the glory of God. There, God punished infidels for their sin, while here Christ enlightened fishermen through his Spirit; there, the confusion of tongues was for the sake of vengeance, while here there was variety so that voices could be joined in unison for the salvation of our souls.[1]

After its worship of the Trinity on the first day of the festival of Pentecost, the Orthodox Church offers the worship of the Holy Spirit on the following day. The icon of the Descent of the Holy Spirit is brought out on this day and it expresses the inner life of the church no less than the icon of the Old Testament Trinity.[2] By "inner life" is meant that life which has already begun its "ascent" through the work of the Holy Spirit. It is a life of inner certainty in the face of outward contradiction, which the author of the Epistle to the Hebrews describes in this way:

What is faith? It is that which gives substance to our hopes, which convinces us of things we cannot see (Hebrews 11:1).

The icon of the Descent of the Holy Spirit seems itself a contradiction inasmuch as Acts 2:1-13 describes the event as one of great pandemonium, so much so that the uninitiated said of the disciples, "They have been drinking too much new wine" (Acts 2:13). The icon expresses a harmony and serenity that seems to belie Luke's description of the event. This is because the icon is addressed to the faithful, who already perceive the inner meaning of the event."[3] Ouspensky says this about the icon, "In contrast to the (icon of)

145

Ascension where the Apostles are gesticulating, here their postures express an hieratic calm, their movements are full of solemnity. They are seated; and some turn a little towards one another, as though talking."[4]

The inner meaning of the event is revealed in the conviction that the Holy Spirit creates, by being present within each member of the Body of Christ, many Christs, that is, many of the Lord's anointed who are on the way to deification.[5] The apostles, who represent the whole Church with its multiplicity of members, here express the spirit of Paul's words to the Corinthians:

> Now the Lord is the Spirit, and where the Spirit of the Lord is, there is freedom. But we all, as with unveiled face we see the Lord's glory as reflected in a mirror, are changed into the same likeness from one degree of glory to another, derived as it is from the Lord who is the Spirit (II Corinthians 3:18).

The four Evangelists are present, holding their Gospels in their hands. The rest hold scrolls as a sign of their having received the gift of teaching.[6] Although the synopticists (Matthew, Mark and Luke) were probably not present at the event, and the apostle Paul was certainly not present, they are present here because the infusion of the Spirit is ongoing, and embraces the whole Church, of which they are a part. Paul and Peter are seated at the head of the circle, respectively on the left and right. The Evangelists are seated next to them, two on either side. The occupied space between Peter and Paul is the place of Christ, the invisible Head of the Body.[7]

At the top of the icon, the heavenly mandorla with its twelve rays depicts the descent of the twelve tongues of fire which rest upon the head of each apostle. These tongues of flame recall the prophecy of John the Baptist that "..he will baptize you with the Holy Spirit and with fire" (Acts 3:11).

In ancient representations of this event, the multitude mentioned in Acts 2:41 was depicted at the bottom of the composition, but soon this multitude was replaced by the figure of a king, whose name, Cosmos, indicates that he represents all the inhabitants of the world. If we as Protestants are troubled by the presence of so unbiblical a figure, Ouspensky comes to our aid by citing a seventeenth century manuscript that mitigates this difficulty:

> Why at the descent of the Holy Spirit is there shown a man sitting in a dark place, bowed down in years, dressed in a red garment with a royal crown on his head, and in his hands a white cloth containing twelve written scrolls? The man sits in a dark place, since the whole world had formerly been without faith; he is bowed down with years, for he was made old by the sin of Adam; his red garment signifies the devil's blood sacrifices; the royal crown signifies sin, which ruled in the world; the white cloth in his hands with the twelve scrolls means the twelve Apostles, who brought light to the world with their teaching.[8]

The icon of the Descent of the Holy Spirit, and the liturgy of the festival, reminds the faithful of the parallel between the confusion of Babel and the symphony or union engendered by the Spirit's Descent:[9]

> When the Most High came down and confused the tongues (in Babel), He divided the nations; but when He distributed the tongues of fire at Pentecost, He called all men to unity. Wherefore we glorify the Holy Spirit with one accord.[10]

The Holy Spirit does not suppress the pluralism and variety of creation for the sake of uniformity. Each individual's experience of the Spirit is unique and part of the symphony of the whole. In the Spirit, division, contradiction and corruption are overcome.[11] "He descended," Ouspensky writes, "upon every member of the Church separately and, although there is 'one and the selfsame Spirit,' 'there are diversities of operation.' "[12] This, of course, reflects Paul's word to the Corinthian Church:

> To one person is given by the Spirit the utterance of wisdom; to another to speak with knowledge according to the same Spirit; to another faith is given by the same Spirit; to another and by the same Spirit the power of healing; to another the working of miracles; to another prophecy; another can test the spirit of the prophets; another can speak in different tongues; another can interpret the tongues. But all these are the work of the same Spirit who distributes to each person exactly as he pleases. I Corinthians 12:8-11.

Pentecost is the affirmation of the multiplicity of persons within the Church.

This theme of union in the midst of diversity may have influenced Orthodoxy's mission to the East as it concerned the question of language. The West, largely for the sake of uniformity, opted for a unified but moribund language, Latin, as the channel for its propagation of the Gospel.[13] If Orthodoxy had a compunction about imposing the Greek language on pagan lands, it certainly must have stemmed in part from its liturgy for Pentecost, and the icon which depicts the Descent of the Spirit. Meyendorff relates a telling vignette comparing the Orthodox to the Latin mission:

> Cyril and Methodius, during their mission to Moravia and their stay in Venice, had several discussions with Frankish missionaries who held 'the heresy of the three languages,' believing that the Gospel could be communicated only in the

three languages used in Pilate's inscription of Jesus' cross: Hebrew, Greek, and Latin. By contrast, Cyril and Methodius stressed that in the East, Slavs, as well as Armenians, Persians, Egyptians, Georgians, and Arabs praised God in their own languages.[14]

Meyendorff speaks of the Spirit as the "symphony" of creation[15] which began with the Spirit of God moving upon the face of the waters. The Spirit, he maintains, does not belong to the category of the miraculous, "but forms a part of the original and natural plan of God. It assumes, inspires and vivifies everything which is still fundamentally good and beautiful, in spite of the Fall."[16] The Spirit holds creation together until this "symphony" is fully realized in the End, or eschatological fulfillment. It is the role of the Church to make this fulfillment approachable through the continuing work of the Spirit.[17] Basil tells us that not only humankind, but nature as a whole will be perfectly itself when in communion with God and filled with the Spirit.[18]

Creation is caught up in the cycle of growth and decay, birth and death. The Church, which has the Holy Spirit as the source of its life, is continually being rejuvenated and renewed. "At a given moment, when the Church has attained to the fullness of growth determined by the will of God, the external world, having used up its vital resources, will perish."[19] Then the Church will be revealed as the true foundation for all creation, for its creatures will be "raised up in incorruptibility to be united to God who will be all in all..."[20]

The idea of growth and ascent in the Spirit is basic to Orthodoxy and, as it happens, in the experience of the Wesleys. The Wesleyan theology of perfection, as we have already indicated, is very close to the Orthodox theology of the ascent, as in this Wesleyan hymn text:

Our needy souls sustain
With fresh supplies of love

Till all thy life we gain
And all thy fullness prove,
And, strengthened by thy perfect grace,
Behold without a veil thy face.[21]

The ascent, which is an ascent of love, never ends. The power of the Holy Spirit is inexhaustible, because God's transcendent being is inexhaustible, "and which, thus, always contains new things to be discovered through the union of love."[22]

1 *Byzantine Daily Worship,* Alleluia Press, PO Box 103, Allendale, NJ., 07401. 1969., p. 894., Eighth tone.
2 Ouspensky, Leonid and Lossky, Vladimir, *The Meaning of Icons,* St. Vladimir's Seminary Press, Crestwood, NY., 10707., 1982., p. 208.
3 Ibid., p. 208.
4 Ibid., p. 207.
5 Lossky, Vladimir, *The Mystical Theology of the Eastern Church,* St. Vladimir's Seminary Press, Crestwood, NY., 10707., 1976., p. 174
6 Op. Cit., Ouspensky and Lossky., p. 207.
7 Ibid., p. 207.
8 Ibid., p. 208., from N. Pokrovsky, The Gospels in *Iconographic Records,* St. Petersburg, 1892., p. 463.
9 Meyendorff, John, *Byzantine Theology: Historical Trends & Doctrinal Themes,* Fordham University Press., NY., 1974., p. 174.
10 Op. Cit., *Byzantine Daily Worship,* p. 891., Kontakion, (eighth tone).
11 Op. Cit., Meyendorff., p. 174.
12 Op. Cit., Ouspensky and Lossky, p. 208., from St. Gregory the Theologian, Discourse 41.
13 Op. Cit., Meyendorff., p. 218.
14 Ibid., p. 218., from Vita Constantini 16, 7-8, in Constantinus et Methodius Thessalonicensis. Fontes, Radovi Instituta 4 (1960) 131.
15 Ibid., p. 174.
16 Ibid., p. 169.
17 Ibid., p. 174.
18 Ibid., p. 169, from *De Spir. S., 16, 38:PG 32:136 B.*
19 Op. Cit., Lossky., p. 178.
20 Ibid., p. 178.
21 *The Methodist Hymnal,* the Methodist Publishing House, Nashville, TN., 164., #315.
22 Op. Cit., Meyendorff., p. 219.

THE DORMITION OF THE VIRGIN

Neither death nor the tomb could hold the Mother of God. She is always ready to intercede for us, forever our steady hope and protection. Since she is the Mother of Life, Christ who dwelt in her ever-virginal womb lifted her up to life.[1]

When I first began this study of iconography, it was not my intention to include the Dormition of the Virgin for what I thought was a logical reason, namely, its inaccessibility to Protestants. Behind this, I must confess, was the growing realization that I hardly knew Mary at all. She had never played a role in my devotional life, and I wasn't given to reading about her. She is given no quarter in most Protestant theological schools and she is rarely mentioned by Protestant theologians. When she is mentioned, it is usually in the context of a discussion of Isaiah 7:14 where it is revealed that the Hebrew word *almah* does not necessarily imply virginity, but refers to a young woman of marriageable age.

If theology in a given context *is* the systematization of popularly held belief or devotion, it does not appear that a Protestant theology of Mary will take root any time soon. Such a theology would have to disregard the "uniqueness" that is ours by virtue of the Reformation. Yet, conversion as we see it means a thoroughgoing transformation of our whole existence — a radical change of heart and mind. This may require a new relationship to preconceived ideas about our identity, culture and tradition, as well as the respective identities, cultures and traditions of other communions within Christ's Church.[2] Conversion must necessarily mean following the continual beckoning of the Spirit wherever it leads. This requires an open mind and an open heart.

To consider iconography only insofar as it excludes any reference to Mary is impossible in any case. It would be like studying in the human body only those organs that do not

155

lead to the heart, and everyone knows that the heart is the organ which animates all the other organs and sustains their life. Mary plays a role analogous to the heart within Eastern Orthodoxy. A study of iconography which attempted to ignore her would, in my opinion, test the beckoning of the Spirit.

The icon of the Dormition of the Virgin embraces two distinct but inseparable moments for the faith of the Orthodox Church: the death and burial of Mary, and her resurrection and ascension.[3] She is seen on her deathbed in the midst of the twelve apostles, mysteriously called to her side from the four winds. In many representations, prominent bishops are also present. The central figure is always the risen Christ who receives the soul of his mother in his arms.[4]

In some representations, the fanatic Athonios has both hands severed by an angel for having had the temerity to attempt to upset her bier. The point here seems to be an argument settled at the Council of Ephesus, (A.D. 431) that Mary was indeed the Mother of God (Theotokos) and not the mother of the man Jesus (Christotokos). Those who would refute this claim do so, it would seem, at their peril.[5] The presence of this figure also discloses that the Dormition, unless contemplated by the inner light of Tradition, is probably inaccessible to those "without."[6]

According to tradition, Mary is the first human being to participate in the final deification of the creature. She represents the firstfruits of the harvest to come.

The Orthodox insist on the term *Theotokos,* that is, Mother of God. "Through her," writes Metropolitan Anthony Bloom, "God became man. He was born into the human situation through her and she is not to us simply an instrument of the Incarnation. She is the one whose personal surrender to God, her love of God, her readiness to be whatever God wills, her humility..is such that God could be born in her."[7]

Just as the Incarnation would have been impossible without the will of the Father, it would have been impossible but for her obedience, expressed in her words, "Here am I, the handmaid of God."[8]

Bloom continues:

> We love her, we feel perhaps in her in a peculiar
> way we see the Word of God spoken by Paul who
> says, 'My power is made manifest in weakness.'
> We can see this frail virgin of Israel, this frail girl,
> defeating sin in her, defeating hell, defeating
> everything by the power of God which is within
> her. And this is why at moments like persecutions,
> when indeed the power of God is made manifest
> in nothing but weakness, the blessed Virgin stands
> out so miraculously, so powerfully in our eyes.[9]

As early as the Second Christian Century, primitive
Christian tradition established a parallel between the Eve of
Genesis 2 and the Mary of Luke's account of the Annunciation. It was a contrast between two virgins. The first sur-
rendered to the serpent's offer of false deification whereas
the second chose acceptance of the will of God."[10]

According to the Orthodox East, the Fall of Adam was
not so complete as it was seen in the Augustinian West. In
the East, original sin, our inheritance from Adam, was seen
as mortality, not guilt. Thus there was never any need to
maintain that Mary received the special grace of immortality.
In the East, the tradition of her assumption, her ascent into
heaven, soul and body, is seen as an anticipation of the
general resurrection to come and a sign of our own deification.[11]

Thomas Merton makes an observation that is certainly
consistent with the Orthodox point of view: "If Mary is
believed to be assumed into heaven, it is because we too are
one day, by the grace of God, to dwell where she is. If
human nature is glorified in her, it is because God desires it
to be glorified in us too, and it is for this reason that his son,
taking flesh, came into the world."[12]

If we Protestants are to put our "protestations" aside, we
may begin to do so by reflecting on her obedience. Merton,

157

himself a Roman Catholic and not Orthodox, may serve as a bridge on this vital issue. He reassures us that Mary is not blessed because of some mythical divine prerogative, but because she has believed in spite of her human limitations. "It is the faith and fidelity of this humble handmaid, 'full of grace' that enables her to be the perfect instrument of God."[13]

Henri Nouwen says of her:

> She knows what it means to be poor, oppressed, a refugee, to be uncertain and confused about the future, to be kept at a distance, to stand under the cross and be the bearer of thoughts and feelings that cannot be shared with anyone.[14]

Further, he says, "She is mother not only to her crucified Son, but to all women and men who suffer in this world."[15]

Mary, for Merton, is transparency itself. She was empty of all egotism and thus as transparent as the glass of a very clean window whose only function is to admit light into the room. When we rejoice in the light we implicitly give praise to the cleanness of the window. And yet, he continues, the Son of God

> ..in emptying Himself of His majestic power, having become a child, abandoning Himself in complete dependence to the loving care of a human mother, in a certain sense draws our attention once again to her. The Light has wished to remind us of the window, because he is grateful to her and because he has an infinitely tender and personal love for her. He asks us to share this love.[16]

If it is commonly believed within Protestant circles that the Orthodox Church holds Mary to be coequal with

Christ, John Meyendorff puts this idea to rest. He tells us that no Council within Orthodoxy has ever made this claim:

> ..the Byzantine Church wisely preserving a
> scale of theological values which always gave
> precedence to the basic fundamental truths of
> the Gospel, abstained from enforcing any
> dogmatic formulation concerning Mary, except
> that she was truly and really the *Theotokos*
> 'Mother of God.'[17]

The journey to Greece, to which I have already referred, included a shore trip to ancient Ephesus on the Turkish mainland. Our group was bussed to the ancient port, now several miles inland. Prior to our return to the ship we stopped at a site I had not realized was on the itinerary, the ancient stone dwelling atop Mount Solmisos known as "the house of the Virgin Mary." Our Turkish guide announced very solemnly that the Theotokos had been brought here by St. John after the crucifixion, and that she had lived in this dwelling the rest of her days.

I quickly referred to the guidebook which said, "A German nun, Anna Catherine Emmerich (1774-1824) saw a vision of this long buried and forgotten cottage. Upon her direction, the area was excavated and the house found."[18] I gave my wife a glance which said, "They've got to be kidding!" and informed her that I had no intention of getting off the bus. Upon her insistence that we rest awhile under the trees, and they were ancient, and drink from the spring ("Even if it's not holy, at least it's cold!") I reluctantly accompanied her to a shaded terrace that afforded a magnificent view of the Turkish plain. Suddenly the idea did not seem so absurd, and this Protestant, not given to meditating on the Theotokos, said, "Why not?"

We Protestants have traveled a long way from the environs of the Reformation, an institution that is not unlike

Ephesus itself. It is a treasure of enormous theological and historical importance, but a ruin, if taken by itself. Ecumenism may be beckoning us, albeit reluctantly, to the heights where the fresh breezes of the Spirit can refresh us and where the water of life is once again fresh and clear.

I left Mt. Solmisos with what I hope remains an open mind and heart. I pray that I am in the process of becoming attuned to mysteries which may once have passed me by.

If the icon of the Dormition of the Virgin is inaccessible to Protestants, it may be because we have not posed the essential question, a question which at this point on the journey may be nothing more than a "Well, why not?"

1 *Byzantine Daily Worship,* Alleluia Press, PO Box 103, Allendale, NJ., 07401. 1969., p. 756., Feast of the Dormition., Kontakion (Second Toen).
2 Wainright, Geoffrey, *Doxology: The Praise of God in Worship, Doctrine and Life,* Oxford University Press., NY., 1980., p. 291.
3 Ouspensky, Leonid and Lossky, Vladimir, *The Meaning of Icons.* St. Vladimir's Seminary Press., Crestwood, NY., 1982., p. 213.
4 Ibid., pps. 213-214.
5 Coniaris, Anthony M., *Introducing the Orthodox Church: Its Faith and Life.,* Light and Life Publishing Co., PO Box 26421, Minneapolis, MN 55426-0421., p. 181.
6 Op. Cit., Ouspensky and Lossky., p. 214.
7 Bloom, Anthony, *Beginning to Pray,* Paulist Press., NY/Ramsey., 1970., pp. 110-111.
8 Ibid., p. 111.
9 Ibid., p. 111.
10 Meyendorff, John, *Byzantine Theology: Historical Trends & Doctrinal Themes,* Fordham University Press., NY., 1974., pp. 146-147.
11 Ibid., p. 147.
12 Merton, Thomas, *New Seeds of Contemplation,* New Directions., 80 Eighth Avenue., NY., 10011., 1962., p. 178.
13 Ibid., p. 170.
14 Nouwen, Henri, J.M., *Behold the Beauty of the Lord: Praying With Icons.,* Ave Maria Press., Notre Dame, Indiana, 46556., p. 36.
15 Ibid., p. 36.
16 Op. Cit., Merton, p. 172.
17 Op. Cit., Meyendorff., pp. 148-149.
18 Gokovali, Dr. Sadan, *Ephesus,* NET., Turistik Yayinlar Sanayi Ve Ticaret A.S., Merkez: Yerebatan Cad. No. 15/3 Sultanahmet, Istanbul., p. 52.

ACKNOWLEDGEMENTS

To the many persons who participated in the completion of this manuscript, I express my heartfelt thanks: John Barns, my friend and mentor; Charles Rohrbacher and Brother Claude Lane of the Mt. Angel Iconographic Institute, for having expanded my understanding of the iconographic technique; Dr. James Logan and Dr. Newell Wert who imparted an appreciation for the discipline of theological thought; Dr. Jay Wesley House, Rev. Tom Webb and Dr. John Piper, my colleagues in ministry, who read the manuscript and offered comments; Dr. Clark Barshinger, whose background in psychology reaffirmed my conviction that all truth is one; and Judy Kauffman, who typed the manuscript.

I am also grateful for the nurture and encouragement I received from the congregation of Zion United Methodist Church, Red Lion, Pennsylvania. Without their support, this book probably would not have been written.

R.M.H.

The author and publisher express their thanks to the following, for their permission to quote from the works listed:

St. Vladimir's Seminary Press, Crestwood, NY: Ouspensky and Lossky, *The Meaning of Icons,* 1982; Kallistos Ware, *The Orthodox Way,* 1980; Vladimir Lossky, *The Mystical Theology and the Eastern Church,* 1976; Leonid Ouspensky, *Theology of the Icon,* 1978; and John Baggley, *Doors of Perception — Icons and their Spiritual Significance,* 1988.

The Morehouse Publishing Company, Wilton, CT, and St. Paul Publications, © 1982, *Mary's Place in Christian Dialogue.*

Alleluia Press, Allendale, NJ: Byzantine Daily Worship, 1969.

Farrar, Straus and Giroux, New York: Alexander Solzhenitsyn, *Stories and Prose Poems,* 1971.

Paulist Press, Mahwah, NJ: Anthony Bloom, *Beginning to Pray.* 1970.

Seabury Press, a division of Harper and Row, San Francisco: Henri Nouwen, *The Way of the Heart* © 1981.

Doubleday, a division of Bantam Doubleday Dell Publishing Group, Inc.: Morrison, Douglas and Nouwen, *Compassion: A Reflection on the Christian Life,* 1982.

New Directions, NY: Thomas Merton, *New Seeds of Contemplation,* 1972.

Fordham University Press: John Meyendorff, *Byzantine Theology: Historical Trends and Doctrinal Themes,* 1979.

Augsburg Fortress Press: Excerpts are reprinted from *I Believe: A Christian's Creed* by Helmut Thielicke, © 1968; and *Festivals and Commemorations* by Philip H. Pfatteicher, © 1980.

Barbara Baker, Houston, TX: for permission to quote from the hymn text, "So Lowly Doth The Savior Ride."

Abingdon Press: Clovis Chappell, *The Seven Words,* 1952; and Martin Schmidt, *John Wesley: A Theological Biography,* Vol. II, part 2, 1973.

INDEX OF BIBLICAL PASSAGES